THE ICICLE
AND THE SUN

THE ICICLE
AND THE SUN

By

William Sansom

REYNAL & COMPANY

NEW YORK

Published by
Reynal & Company
New York

Contents

Illustrations

ix

ILLUSTRATIONS

Acknowledgements for permission to reproduce photographs are due to the following: Inga Aistrup Foto for 'Kronborg Castle', 'Amalienborg Palace' and 'Nyhavn'; Sven Türck for 'Copenhagen Fishmarket' and 'Danish Chimney-Sweep'; K. Rasmussen for 'Horse-drawn Lifeboat'; the Danish Tourist Bureau for 'Aabenraa, South Jutland'; the Carlsberg Brewery for 'Townscape with Elephants'; Jonals Co., Copenhagen, for 'Landscape with Cows'; the Swedish Tourist Traffic Association for 'Stockholm' and 'Göta Canal'; Th. Christiansson for 'Aby Trotting Track'; the Nationalmuseum, Stockholm, for 'Swedish Sphinx'; K. W. Gullers for 'Swedish Manor'; J. Allan Cash for 'Leksand Longboat' and 'Bergen Funicular'; Berndt Klyvare for 'Play-Sculpture'; the Finnish Embassy for 'Forest Timberman' and 'Salla Church'; Kuvaosasto for 'Helsinki Harbourline', 'Tilka Military Hospital' and 'Steam Bath'; the Finnish Tourist Association for 'Vehoniemi Ridge'; Suoman Kansallismuseo for 'Grandmother Clock'; the Press and Foreign Information Office, Royal Norwegian Embassy, for 'Oslo Waterfront', 'Lofoten Fishing Fleet', 'Borgund Stave-Church', and 'Hardanger Fjord'; K. Harstad for 'Vigeland's Howling Child'; H. A. Amundsen for 'Reindeer'.

INTRODUCTION

PERVERSITY bought me my first ticket north. Too constant a song of the olive south, where real lemons grow on trees and the sapphire sea is hot as a bath, suggested that all this, nice as it is, had become overstressed. The outsider inside began to niggle and I took a ticket in the opposite direction.

Up above and round the Baltic lay a familiar shape on the map known too shapelessly in the mind as Scandinavia-and-Finland. Butter, matches, Lapps and Vikings, one might roughly think; giant blonde houris and huge grey business men. But there must be more to it than that? It began to seem almost impertinent, certainly disproportionate, to know so little about four separate national entities making up such a large part of Europe. So I bought this ticket, and embarked on a ship with a Christmas tree lashed to the masthead and a few blond giants already *snaps*-happy—and came the next day in sight of my first Scandinavian landmark, one of the largest fish-ball factories in Europe, at Stavanger. Thus, it all began at the beginning.

But the bit between the teeth I went on and travelled all around, returning several times in summer and winter, by sea and by air, always amazed and enchanted by landscapes and weathers and manners different from those of the rest of Europe. This book is the result.

One of my present purposes is to try to differentiate between these four countries, Denmark, Sweden, Finland and Norway—so that they may be considered as truly distinct from each other as other European countries whose culture is roughly similar, as distinct as Belgium from France, Portugal from Spain, Austria from Bavaria. It is often by the lesser architectures—the shapes of cafés, the colours of local paint, the doorknobs and the uniforms of police and postmen—that we know in which country we sit. Ideally, I would like to find some terms by which I could be sure that, set down in a café in Helsinki or Copenhagen or Oslo or Stockholm I would know, apart from recognizing guide-book architecture and idiomatic signs, where I was. But no such system can be exact, for the truth is that though each of these cultures is distinct, there is much in common between them. However, sitting in a station café in Geneva you know very well you are not in a similar café in Dijon. Why? Detail. There is a lot that is cleaner, greyer, more rubber-tyred than in browner, lacier, dustier, zinc-countered France. The passing porter has a different-coloured smock. There are likely to be waitresses, not waiters. And so on. It is the sum of much detail, the smell and sound and taste of daily life that together compose the label.

The north, as you get to know it, offers similar small distinctions. If the people seem to be gobbling a kind of Yorkshire-Dutch and the next-door woman is smoking a cigar and most of the houses are built of brick or faced with plaster, you may know you are in Denmark. If they are speaking what sounds like a kind of Spanish-Italian language and the next-door table is drinking gin-and-grape-fruit and you feel you saw something Russian a moment before (a droshki, a vodka bottle, blini on a plate), then undoubtedly it is Helsinki. If you are sitting by a deep red wood building in the country, and there are firs and birch about—you may be in Finland or Sweden or Norway: but look at those high mountains behind—not Finland: and look at the neat white palings round the house, probably not Sweden. A short beige horse walks by—and the total is likely to be Norway.

Broadly speaking, you may say that the Danes are easy-going and light-hearted, the Swedes grave and passionate, the Finns earth-bound and near-mystic, the Norwegians active and bluff with a touch of Celtic wildness. But only broadly—there will not be many days before an exception reduces the rule. And one may broadly add that the flat appearance of brick-built Denmark is North German; and that Norway feels like Sweden with a touch of Danish ease; that Finland is also like Sweden, but with here and there a garnish of old Russian influences. Broadly one will be right: with again too many exceptions to prove the rule. For broad rules are not the kernel of this matter: what is important is the sum total of many small details—and it is this that, in such an impressionistic book, I have tried to convey.

Politically and socially these four countries are slowly merging. They rightly want to keep together and to lower their barriers. Passports are no longer registered, permits to work next door are not necessary. In many other ways they are co-operating. The only truly serious obstacle to this mutual ideal has been raised by the different military positions and affiliations of each individual nation : but otherwise the direction and will for co-operation is paramount. Thus, in stressing the distinctions rather than the similarities of Scandinavia-and-Finland, I may seem to be barking up a wrong tree. But I do not think so. The pattern of the world grows more monotonous each day—uniformity is the unfortunate price of cultural toleration and ease of communication. But there is already a reaction, or at least a rearguard action. Already in many European countries regional differences are becoming prized and preserved, even discovered, for the first time. To go air-hopping across Europe—say from London to Helsinki, landing at Amsterdam and Hamburg—one is struck by the similarity of airports. There are good reasons why such buildings and runways should look the same, for they are an essentially contemporary development—just as it was reasonable in a commonly romantic period to find the architecture of most nineteenth-century railway terminals, though much decorated, largely interchangeable. But arriving at those steam terminals you tasted instantly on the platforms the peculiar life of the city at which you had arrived—the customs and habits and smells of the city invaded the platforms. It is not so with the airport. Apart from slight differences in the food and a few climatic differences in clothes, it is all much the same. You have to narrow your eyes too subtly to appreciate very minor shades of difference, which is an amusing game but a sad one. The life of airports is international. And this monotonous air, hinted at for years in the more luxurious hotels, is spreading.

INTRODUCTION

Attempts to revive national features, like dressing waitresses in peasant costumes, usually fail. What one must cling to are the living remnants; and they are usually to be found, pleasantly matured, in the residue of patterns of life left over from the last large span of years from the final decades of the nineteenth century up to the beginning of the Kaiser's War.

This is not to suggest that one should be only and forever yearning backwards. That is an addiction which soon becomes a malady. And it would be particularly silly to suggest it of countries so decidedly progressive and radical as these four. But at least, while they last, it seems worth while to cast an occasional eye on, and enjoy for the last time, the older passing distinctions.

Turning for a moment from the idea of differences to the many similarities between these countries, I notice one particular pitfall in these four accounts. In one I might emphasize schooling, in another ski-ing, in another the happy coloured multitude of the children about. Such matters and many others are often interchangeable. But too much repetition had to be avoided. I could not go on repeating the common love for indoor plants, or telling about the pianist who usually accompanies your dinner so soulfully that at first you can hardly bear to eat— though finally you eat with greater relish because food becomes a *compensation*.

One further and technical point has been the difficulty of always writing Scandinavia-*and*-Finland. Finland is not properly Scandinavia, but where I have used that cloudy word Scandinavia, Finland is usually implied as well. Also there is the technical question of Scandinavian and Finnish—there we go again—words which have the definite article suffixed e.g. Studenterlunden, the *en* meaning 'the'. If sometimes it seems that the English article is omitted, it is, it is to be hoped, for this reason alone.

Finally, I would like to express my gratitude for all the kindness and generosity, official and unofficial, extended to me by the people of these four countries: and to make my grateful acknowledgement to the editors of the American periodical *Holiday* by whom the first three of these chapters, in a slightly contracted form, were once commissioned and first published.

W. S.

Kronborg Castle at Elsinore, with the courtyard where *Hamlet* is performed

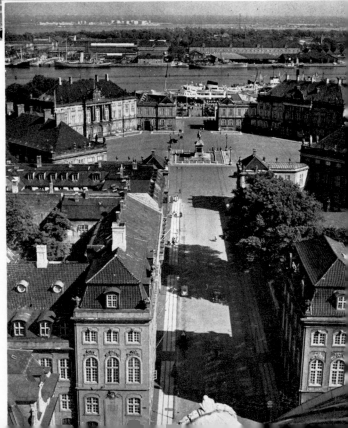

quadriform Royal ace of Amalienborg the quayside at enhagen

Nyhavn Canal, whose many-coloured houses contain a famous
line of sailors' bars

The live fish market in the centre of Copenhagen

DENMARK

I

DENMARK

GIANT pink horses, cigar-smoking spinsters, blood-red cottages with green plush roofs, ships in the streets, five hundred islands, a sky-line of bottles and a capital with a twenty-four-hour-day night-life. . . . These at random are some of the ingredients of a country which is too often loosely thought of as a flat green conveyor belt endlessly sending forth model eggs and bacon and butter; or too vaguely embraced as 'part of Scandinavia'. But royally democratic Denmark is part of nothing but itself, it is a national entity jealous of its character and customs, properly peculiar.

Just as there is no purely original artist, but a man who produces a fresh and visionary work from an amalgam of selected influences—so with a country. Broadly shaped by climate, its character and originality are what it selects from its history and its neighbours; it is the digestion and recreation of these that forms, like the shuffling of a vast and intricate kaleidoscope of taste and endeavour and time, the original pattern we find as the customs barrier is passed and a new flag—in this case the red and white standard of Denmark—replaces all others.

Denmark is in many ways a middle land. It lies on a latitude with Labrador and a longitude almost as far east as Berlin. It is thus not truly northern, no iceland of winterlong snow and fir forest like its Scandinavian neighbours; nor is it properly separated from the teutonic influences of the south Baltic coast. Nevertheless you will see snow-ploughs waiting in the railway sidings; and any attempt to use a German dictionary will be confounded by a language wild with øs and æs and aas. Our human, parcel-loving minds like to try to align national character: but if one tries to make the Dane into a Swede or Norwegian, one finds he is as far apart from the formal graces of the first as from the athletic brio of the latter. The Dane is an easy-going broad-living fellow. And if, alternatively, one searches to the south, and tries to relate him with that relatively easy-going kind of German, the Rhinelander—there again the trip-rope rises, for the Rhinelander's ease is largely Catholic and wine-growing, and the Dane is nationally Lutheran and a beerdrinker. They are simply not similar.

The Dane, with his large sense of humour, his imagination, his independence yet his ideal of co-operation, remains distinct. The key to him most probably lies in another direction altogether, in the word 'skipper', which is in the first place the Danish for master of a ship and only secondly the borrowed property of the whole English-speaking world. For Denmark, with its living scattered over hundreds of islands, and its position at the head of the Baltic and abreast the North Sea, is essentially a seafaring nation, the salt sea is in the winds and in the bone. Travelling about the inland sea-roads on the ferry, among witchlike buoys mounted with brooms and past churches in which always hang model ships, it will be seen suddenly that the green sea is rather greener than usual, that a green wave humps up a little too solidly to be water, that it is in fact not water but green turf suckled by the sea, grassland of a low-lying island, and one more evidence of this wide integrity of little pieces, purple earth and green grass and blue sea, that still goes by the old name of its southern mainland border, the march of the Danes, Denmark. It is bright, fresh and lively sea country—neither rugged and keen like Norway, nor low and drenched like Holland, nor built on the ice-age rock of Sweden: this is soft, sandborn country, freshened by sea winds, lively—and the broad character of a people is seldom divisible from what lies beneath its feet.

A bewildering map shows Denmark as, very roughly, three pieces of land divided by two vertical sea-belts. To the left Jutland, springing from the mainland of Europe: in the middle, the rich cluster called Fünen (Fyn): and to the right Zealand and its islands, with the capital Copenhagen. Of four million Danes, one million live in Copenhagen: so whether you arrive by sea from England to Jutland, or from Germany to Zealand, or via the North Pole to Kastrup airport, the capital must finally be the place of destination and, for present purposes, our right point of departure.

Copenhagen—or as the Danes with a northerly bite have it, København—is a salt-sea city where deep-draught steamships berth hard up against the main streets. Through the delicate rococo quarter-

ings of the Royal Amalienborg Palace, there can be
seen the giant red and black funnel of an ocean-
going liner, painted steel bright against the
weathered grey pediments: the King, a sailor himself and monarch of a democracy, can, and does,
wave from his balcony as these great ships sail off
into the Baltic night. As you wander among the
gracious old houses by the quays, past great Christiansborg Castle that houses the Government, and
then through much of the centre of this city—it
seems that there is a ship at the end of every second
street. Against a graceful copper spire the rigging of
sailboats describes a sharp calligraphy that in other
cities would be made by the winter branches of a
tree; and on the green lawns of the Rosenborg park,
white seagulls strut the part of pigeons. There is a
seaman's roll about the place. Streets quickly turn
into bollarded quays; and into the main square of
Kongens Nytorv, where among old mansions the
Royal Theatre stands, there debouches the dockful
of jazzed and tarted sailors' dives called Nyhavn—
as if Hoboken led off Times Square or Limehouse
lay by Piccadilly.

Ships. And spires. The copper spires of Copenhagen are the city's other fable. Castles, churches,
and other buildings of eminence vie to strike with
bright verdigris the grey winter sky, the summer's
high blue: these green writhings are dreamlike as
the ships—the spire of the copper-roofed Bourse is
made up of dragon's tails entwined upwards to end
in a point of unique delicacy, the spire of Christians-
havn Church wreathed with a gilded copper stair-
case spiralling to the sky, the spire of the Russian

Church spangles its three great onion bulbs over the high roofs of Bredgade, Christiansborg and the Nicolai Church topple giant crowns and high gilded balls dizzily to the heavens. Stand at a high window and see these green and gold towers and spires appearing and disappearing in the weaving of a morning mist, one moment gilded by the sun, the next suddenly vanished—and one may feel properly diminutive among a race of immense and decorous chessmen striding formally, gravely, the streets of a dream.

But beneath the spires lies the real city, and one that well lives up to its familiar pseudonym, the Paris of the North. Copenhagen is a most light-hearted city compared with its heavier northern neighbours. A Parisian frivolity laces the rococo of some of the older buildings, when they are not too Dutch; the air is bright, an enlivening clarity glasses the northern sunlight and—an unequivocal fact—the opportunity to dance and drink continues throughout the twenty-four hours. To test this, first take your dinner in one of the large music-halls, such as the Atlantic Palace or Lorry—or in those world-famous Tivoli gardens. You will sit in a restaurant of grand dimension, serving perhaps a thousand diners, and see a creditable variety-performance (Copenhagen has a particular reputation for this, a good billing in Copenhagen ensures interest in an artiste throughout the big music-halls of Central and Northern Europe): you can stay and dance, or go to one of a dozen more intimate restaurants: at one or two o'clock, carry on to a night-club such as the Adlon (entrance via your passport and a few *kroner*) : when this closes at five or so in the morning other restaurants with music, such as Hanegalet (The Cock's Crow) or Jomfruburet (The Maiden's Bower) conveniently open their doors : by eleven or so in the morning there will be bands playing for you to dance to in one or other of the small bars in Nyhavn : fit in thereafter a tea-dance somewhere, followed by an aperitif dance at some such place as Wonder Bar, and you are ready for the Atlantic Palace again.

Tivoli demands special mention. Generally in Europe the more graceful tradition of the pleasure garden has fallen away : but here still, in the centre of a capital city, is a large enclosed garden, planted with trees and harbouring its own idyllic lake, where one may enjoy a variety of pleasures—a fine orchestra, a performance of the Commedia dell' Arte, a military band, a number of excellent restaurants and thereafter all the fun of the usual fair. But it is a place much removed from the raucous pleasure-drome of modern conception : and although it boasts a switchback and bright-lighted booths, it still remains a tree-shaded pleasance where the best may be enjoyed for little money among a pleasure-strolling crowd not much removed in spirit from those earlier Copenhageners who first frequented these gardens to the enlivening measure, the 'madly racing strains', of the celebrated *Champagne Gallop*.

To those days, too, belong a few of the older and still well-preserved restaurants and taverns, such as Café à Porta and Hviid. A Porta, standing across from the Royal Theatre, glitters with brass hat-pegs and gold lincrusta-ed walls. Its chandeliers and rows of champagne bottles, its old gilded eagles and faience pots and tasselled curtains present as much of a plush panache as ever was managed by Budapest or Baden Baden: its table-cloths are thick and white, cigar-smoke rises comfortably from red-plush alcoves (many women smoke cigars too)—it is certainly one of the few perfectly preserved nineteenth-century cafés left in Europe. Across the road lies the chain of cellars and dark drinking-rooms called Hviid, the oldest tavern in Copenhagen, where wine or beer or a glass of *snaps* goes well with dark wood and old walls, a sense of arrested time and the taste of lee-musty barrels in the air. Krog's fish restaurant on the cobbled quay by Christiansborg is another place of old, well-tried establishment, serving fish fresh from the live fish market on its doorstep at a table for connoisseurs. (And here and in other restaurants it is well for the gourmet not to head straight for the lobster section, but to lend a tongue to the simple plaice: it is a speciality of the country, and excellent.)

Serene and ample relics, these: but most of Copenhagen's better restaurants are designed in a modern manner, comfortable, and on the whole aesthetically successful. Two concessions to the modern manner, however, the restaurateur will not make—he refuses the usual brittle chair confected for a dwarf poodle, and insists on something that will sustain a roundly ample Danish ham; and he refuses to limit the amount of food on the plate—so that still, in a world of diet and calculation, you are given the kind of plateful that does honour to the eye. A decision to take the national *sømrrebrød*, or table of cold assorted foods, will bring you first a trayful of seven different kinds of herring, sweet-pickled, sour-pickled, smoked, soused, salted and so on, with several salads and pickled vegetables to choose from; and then a second tray bearing a dish each of smoked eel, smoked salmon, fried plaice, fried eel, roast veal, spiced ham, cured ham, hard eggs, scrambled eggs, egg salad, shrimps in mayonnaise, tongue, roast beef, salami sausage, beetroots and cucumbers, liver pâté, orange salad and cold roast pork. This will be followed by a little something hot, something to warm an empty corner—mock turtle meat with fish balls, or perhaps a veal cutlet in sherry sauce. The entirety will cost a dozen *kroner*, if that. It is a popular misconception that the Danes face up to this every day: not even they could manage it. More usual for them to select for a light meal one or two of the above, laid on buttered bread. Or to try perhaps *frickadellar*— appetizing little meat balls: or *biksemade*—a dicing of meat and richly fried potatoes: or, as always the delicious plaice (*rødspætte* or 'red spot') cooked in fresh butter.

Much of Copenhagen, like its food and its big bastioned castles, has a solid blustering quality despite its light air, its rococo, its aerial modern flats radiating through the suburbs. Many of the central older shops are cellar-shops set down below the pavement away from the winter cold: gilt lettering on black glass richens the façades, and often an old sign —a wooden pretzel for a baker, a surgeon's silver bleeding bowl for a barber—swings outside in the wind . . . as two enormous strawberry horses with

flowing manes rumble a brewer's dray over the cobbles, as a scarlet-coated postman rides his bicycle by,
as chimes from a church spire ring out a sad little
silvered tune, as wood and cigar smoke spice the air,
as mute well-fed gulls circle about the fish-wives
gutting on the fish-quay, as ferries draw out to canals
and islands, as a hammering from shipyards echoes
across the wide harbour to where the Little Mermaid
spreads her tail on her rock to charm her visitors, as
the city's silent cycle-life pedals to and fro and an old
man winds his pipe-organ and the loud little band
of the Royal Guards marches daily to its doll duty at
the Palace . . . but cities are endless, and Copenhagen is as various as any other capital with its offering of parks and museums, great shops and small
kiosks, its wide tram-belling thoroughfares and its
quiet corners among the older streets . . . one can
only pick at random—the Glyptotek, rich with
sculpture and a momentous iron-pillared palm garden, with its fine collection of French impressionists
that includes among much else Manet's terrifying
Absinthe Drinker . . . or the crown jewels in rosy
Rosenborg palace disappearing from view as the
pilfering hand extends across an invisible beam . . .
or a performance of the Royal Ballet at the gold and
cream Royal Theatre with its richly mirrored pro-
menades and that formidable gilded message above
the proscenium EI BLOT TIL LYST (*Not only for pleasure*)
. . . or this or that or the hundred philological sur-
prises that erupt on all sides: STOP FOR BLINK says the
traffic light (*stop when the light blinks*), HJAELP yells the
security button in the lift (*help*), GOD MAD announces
a restaurant (*good food*) . . . such terrors as FYSISK can

be reduced phonetically to a simple 'physical', and TOBAKKER makes nice baby-talk for 'tobaccoes'. But half the Copenhageners speak English, there is no real need to worry and the language can be left to delight the eye.

The coast-road to Elsinore takes you out and north, past the startling skyscape of empty bottles piled up outside the Tuborg brewery, along by villas and small estates set among gardens and birches and the first of Copenhagen's bathing beaches at Klampenborg, which offers such diverse distractions as a race-course and tuna-fishing. A Copenhagener can be out of his office and in the sea within half-an-hour. Beaches and a residue of small fishing villages line the waters of a tideless Sound, and across the way lies the coast of Sweden. Perhaps now for the first time one realizes the wideness of life on these flatlands, how much more immense the sky becomes, with life a pinprick beneath a consciously curved dome of blue and endless air. Here you can breathe. In the immediate distance rise the fairy storeys of Kronborg, Hamlet's Castle. Despite a levity of romantic turrets and Dutch gabling, this is a monster fortress and one can well see how its cannon for so many years weighed an iron stopper into this bottleneck of the Baltic. Ferries to Sweden from here: and popular, for by Elsinore lies Marienlyst, a large beach-hotel that runs the only gaming-tables permitted in the whole of Scandinavia—the Swede who wants to drink freely and ruin himself at the limit of ten *kroner* is a hungry week-end visitor. Even the

Swedish elk, a beast of intractable size and truly of
the North, has been known to swim across.

Inland lies peaceful green wooded country, the
royal deer forests round Lake Esrom and the lovely
palace of Fredensborg, a white and classic edifice
with roofs of a brilliant dark blue tile. This is the
autumn residence of the royal family: and it was
here that King Christian IX, known as the Father-
in-Law of Europe for the number of daughters he
provided for her scattered thrones, used to entertain
on his lawns the Tsar of Russia, the Empress Dag-
mar, the Prince of Wales, Princess Alexandra and
so many others of the related royal families and
courts of Europe. And it is here that one might
realize the curious insistence of blue in the Danish
colourscape. On an autumn day, against green lawns
and the tawn and gold of great beeches, those royal
dark blue tiles, glazed and richly brilliant, stand
insistent against a sky of paler blue; and alone in the
park two guards approach, black bearskins and pale-
blue trousers. Blue hits sharply against the greens of
nature: it is this insistent wink of blue—on uniforms,
in the Royal Porcelain, in the bright clothes of children, in the sky, in the sea, in blonde eyes, and
always in that subtle blue of the roof tiles—that in its
very unorthodoxy seems more to mark the country
than its natural colours of purple earth and green
field and even the ubiquitous red and white flag.
Colours are important. The pleasures of travel lie
not only in the enjoyment of strange excellencies,
but also in a feeling for strange detail: and here
colours, and small daily habits, the way the doorknobs move and how the sugar is wrapped, can be in

total more impressive than isolated instances of fine
architecture and distinguished landscape. What
more Italian than the papery flutter of those giant
lire notes? What more Danish than the big brass
coins, with their feeling of plain *money*, tokens and
unprecious, brassy binnacle brass and brass of the old
castle chest, felt in the pocket nowhere else? The
windows of every house in Denmark are jungled with
green plants, such as mother-in-law's-tongues, that
thrive in steam heat; like sky-blown angels the
builders wear white caps and white overalls and
decorate the skeleton rafters with flags and wreaths;
the six-seater taxis are shaped like chars-a-banc and
called 'half-a-loaf-of-rye-bread', coffee is drunk with
cream not milk and a white eiderdown serves for
blankets and there is *always* a bicycle behind you and
the postboxes are yellow and the King is called a
Kong.

South to Hillerød—and to yet another castle.
With Rosenborg, Christiansborg, Amalienborg,
Kronborg, and Fredensborg the sixth great palace or
castle within an hour's drive of Copenhagen. Fre-
deriksborg is again built of red brick in the Dutch
renascence style. It stands on a lake, and, moated
and doubled in its own placid water, may serve as
the epitome of all these other Danish castles and fortified manor houses that give this small democracy
so aristocratic an air, resonant jewels of past feudal
wealth studding the co-operative farmlands. A castle
in Denmark has a special magic: no Rhenish crag
to lend it drama, no confluence of surging rivers,

no frowning mountain pass—simply, it rises from land that is level for miles around, and, enmoated, sleeps. Seen from a distance its turrets, gilded by the low lanternlike northern sun, play the magic of a mirage: or discovered in a wooded grove, it breathes the inward-dreaming sleep of something more enchanted than perhaps it is. For these massive walls were built for trouble—they can reek of the bad, as with the beautiful castle at Egeskov, one of whose masters walled up his living daughter, and all these other dark oubliettes from the pretty days when women were buried alive for theft and adultery was rewarded by a quick divorce of the head from the body.

South of Copenhagen, near but not too near the airport of Kastrup, lies the little seatown Dragør, a cobbled and narrow-streeted port of frigate days whose roofs are emboldened by streaks of white cement, that like white surf and gull-droppings, match so well the sea. With Dragør there is completed, within the radiation of a mild hour from Copenhagen, a comfortable cross-section for the three-day visitor of much of greater Denmark: castles, lakes, forest-land, thatched farmsteads, dunes, and the pervasive sea. But of course it is only a taste: this country, though relatively so small, is diverse enough to deserve a deeper draught. And first, a crossing over the Great Belt to the rich farmlands of Fünen, where flowering lilac hedges the fields and white churches, their façades built in the form of steps, mark a hopeful ascent to the heavens.

These curious churches rise from the flat like giant-piped organs; and sometimes, in their square-stepped whiteness, appear almost like Arab confections placed surreally here in a soft green northern desert. The farmhouses again have bright green roofs—a most vivid and luminous moss lays its plush over the purplish mole-coloured thatch—and beneath this the walls will be washed with blood-red ochre or left to a white and black, precisely squared, half-timbering. They are wide low buildings built in a square surrounding an inner courtyard. The family lives in one wing of the square, while pigs, cows and horses occupy the others. The pigs one sees about are so pink and clean that they might easily be thought to sleep in beds and sit to table, Disney creatures: and the cows, good fat butter-beef, often set a Frisian black and white about the fields to match the black and white half-timbering: but of all this surprisingly unmuddled and well-kempt beast-life, the horses are by far the most prepossessing—tall, heavy, heraldic creatures, their nut-brown hides are often topped with a mane of long and lovely blonde hair through which mischievously peers a solitary, brown, langourous eye: they have all the coquetry of enormous sun-burned blondes, and, for horses, look excessively naked.

Svenborg in the south of this middle part of Denmark is a dull but comfortable springboard from which one may visit again a number of manor-houses and in particular the smaller islands depending from Fünen. The large Christiansminde summer-hotel two kilometres outside Svenborg faces Taasinge Island whose lovely beech-woods, preserved by the state, grow gracefully to the sea's edge. The beech with its grey elephant hide and its nutty leaf, quick to yellow in autumn, is Denmark's national tree—

Traditional Danish chimney-sweep

Horse-drawn lifeboat on Fanø Island

Steep-pitched roofs of Aabenraa, South Jutland

Townscape with elephants—the Carlsberg Brewery offices

Landscape with cows

not the Scandinavian fir whose indigenous growth ends with the Skagerrak—and the national anthem rightly lauds its lovely wedding with the sea, green leaves in consort with the salt. Valdemar's Slot (castle), but more mansion than castle, stands on Taasinge, its roof pitted with windows gazing heavy-lidded over a flowered lake and down wooded vistas reaching to the sea: a skipper's island retreat, enjoyed by the naval hero Niels Juel, and a fine essay in sumptuous tranquillity.

These are properly seafaring islands, they sing with the salt. Aerø, whose magic name is echoed by its Hotel Harmonien—as if Prospero himself had conjured these from the sea—has a fine old well-preserved town of sea-men's cottages and burghers' mansions. Its witchy little houses with their eye-level roofs come straight from a child's book of fairytales. A *trompe-l'œuil* of red and white bricks is painted between leaning timbers; walls are washed lilac with chestnut beams, others green, yellow, crimson—on paper as sickly as a sunset, but to wander among most real, and resonant of time, weather, and the last landfall. Another skipper in retreat here—Peter Jacobsen, an eighty-year-old round-the-worlder—sits in charge of a museum of ships and ships in bottles. Five hundred ships, and none the same, reads the prospectus. The old rooms are crowded with models of every kind of ship, from a fourteen-master Swedish iron-ore carrier to an Iceland outrigger, from whalers to junks to dhows to barques and barquantines in all diverse rig—indeed these rooms plastered with postcards and letters to Peter from all over the world (you only have to draw a ship in a

c

bottle and put Denmark on the envelope) make the world and a lifetime seem small.

'Umpteen *kroner*', old Jacobsen muttered, 'a bottle of brandy costs now. When I was a boy it cost twenty-five *øre*, and nobody thought twice about drinking two bottles a day.'

Silence in the old room shadowed with ships. Time ticked. But at last the old man sighed and turned away, adding casually, as one might brush away a fly:

'Of course, there was more drunkenness then.'

Fünen has Odense, and Odense had Hans Christian Andersen. No use omitting the 'Christian' in Denmark: Andersens are multitude, as are Nielsens and Jensens, Hansens and so on. Initials or christian names must be used, and the great storyteller becomes 'H.C.' which sounds in Danish very like 'Horsey', which in turn fits too aptly old Andersen's face itself. This extraordinary man, with his great coarse features and his giant hands and feet, deeply sensitive of these and of his early poverty, turned directly from the lathe of that sensitivity all the great tenderness and love that illuminate his work: a not unusual process with writers, but one which makes this big nervous man, who always travelled with a rope to hang outside his bedroom window in case of fire, and who kept by his bedside a note demanding a thorough awakening in case he was thought to be dead and thus in danger of being buried alive (Poe's claustrophobic horror)—makes him into a much more interesting character than the common misconception of a kindly old top-hatted gentleman enclustered with children. He did not, in fact, much like children; and insisted on their exclusion from the design of a statue of himself. In Odense stands the house of his birth, an H. C. Andersen museum, and everywhere, hallowed, seats upon which he sat.

Connection between all these islands has hitherto been made by ferry—broad car-carrying ships, bearing their two tall funnels abreast to loom from the pewter mists like Mississippi steamboats, and in their varnished brown planking echoing some of the gentle melancholy of a painting by Tissot. But now an end to these. Now Jutland (Jylland), the third and largest sector of the country—and a firm steel bridge as presage of what is ahead, an upward turn of the firm mainland of Europe.

The picture changes. The land is still farmed as effectively as possible. But a very large part of Jutland is heath country, and gives the lie to the popular impression that Denmark is a land where every neat green inch is turned into meat and milk. Firs are imported to combat the sandy growth of heather and heath plants: firs act as wind and snow breaks among the fields. In Jutland rise the Raebild hills, presented as a National Park by Danish Americans. Here a copy of Lincoln's log cabin home, built of logs sent from all over the U.S.A., houses a museum of Danish-American emigration where thousands of Danes and Americans gather each year to applaud Independence Day.

There is a windswept sense of wildness about Jutland. Whether it is in these rolling hilly heaths; or at the very tip of the northernmost Skaw where the

waters of two seas meet and wrestle over submerged
sand-dunes, and where the spire of an old church
rises from the dunes to mark forever where a great
sandstorm once submerged the main body; or on the
flat marsh-districts of the North Sea to the West, a
place of great dykes and again sand-dunes making a
lunar landscape of strange little hills—and where
islands like Fanø offer eighteen kilometres of broad
clean white sand for the pleasure of summer bathers,
and in winter echo the thundering of the hoofs of a
team of great Jutland horses dragging the life-boat
out to sea, wild-maned in the lightning, legendary.

And Jutland claims the woodland lake district
round Silkeborg, placid waters for yacht or canoe,
and for the ninety-year-old paddle-steamer that
still winds its way along tree-roofed canals or across
broad lake waters beneath the eminence of the Sky-
Mountain. This is Denmark's five-hundred-foot-
high [*sic*] mountain whose summit does indeed feel
strangely sky-bound among the immense flat views
extending on all sides. Further south, near the German border, stands the old marsh-town of Ribe,
whose quays have so often been lost deep beneath
the flooding sea, whose cathedral has been inun-
dated, and where Egyptian storks arrive to nest on
the roofs each year, always, they swear, on the same
date to a day. And on Jutland lies the ancient turf of
Jelling, where the burial mounds of old King Gorm
and his wife rise to remind one, with their great Runic
stones, of the ancient character of this land and bring
a shiver of possibility into the old admonition: 'Seek
not to seduce another's wife with the alluring charms
of Runic incantations.' The names of Gorm, Harald

DENMARK

Bluetooth and Sven Forkbeard, like other Dark Age figures such as Pippin of Aquitania, have a comic ring and make fun of ages that were very dark and bloody indeed. These people were real and most formidable—like the muscular bishop whose bones cleft by a battle-axe you can still see at Øm, and like the Grauballe man, a pagan sacrificial victim preserved unputrified for two thousand years in peat, whose well-tanned skin embellishes the museum at Aarhus. There, in fact, lies a man intact after two thousand years: the present King of Denmark can claim direct descent from the first Christian King Gorm, A.D. 900. Denmark is old.

But new, too. Industry has compelled into being such cities as Aalborg with its great *akvavit* distilleries: and Aarhus, whose fine new University and well-wooded planning present a spacious and hopeful outlook for the modern industrial city; and Esbjerg, the arrival port from the English passage, which less than a hundred years ago was a hamlet of twenty persons and now has nearly fifty thousand inhabitants to man a large fishing fleet of pale blue smacks and manage the heavy butter-and-bacon trade for England and elsewhere.

This highly developed trade in dairy-farm produce comes from a new outlook in Danish farming. Danish farms are mostly small-holdings run individually by their owners, hard-working and 'dirty-boot', but who have also developed among themselves a high degree of co-operation, centralizing all such matters as sterilization and marketing, consulting together on new techniques, combining without being collective—an attitude that allows for a high degree of efficiency yet leaves the man on his own land in free possession of his soul.

The old and the new, the scientifically packed and frozen butter deriving from a venerable thatched farmhouse—again we find that easy, sensible admixture, that middle way which, like its middle-status between the true North and the European main, makes Denmark so difficult to define, so amiable to encounter. A land of sun-charmed castles and tall silver oil-tanks, a royal democracy whose king sits one moment on the ritual throne and the next conducts the orchestra publicly in the pit of his Royal Theatre. A country where every time you drink a glass of beer you know you are doing somebody somewhere some good—for lager and learning go hand in hand, all the Carlsberg profits are devoted to educational or artistic foundations or to general scientific research. A land where criminal alcoholics are ordered a most fitting but elsewhere unusual corrective: the anti-alcoholic drug, Antabus. A country whose main railway station in Copenhagen is rich with stained glass and chandeliers but has no trains in it—they run underneath—and where a day's run might land you up against an eel-farm, an archipelago, a stork's nest, or a brewer's office mounted on two life-size stone elephants: or in a sudden village of green weather-boarding built by Dutch pirates, or near the abrupt rise of Møn's white cliffs, ghosts of otherwise flat seas, or on a wild shore where crofters still collect the sea-drift amber, or at a large inn (*kro*) by a troutstream, or in an extremely comfortable hotel in a modern town of progressive excellence. Or anywhere else in a diverse land of hard-working people who refuse to take themselves too seriously, whose government began and has for years subsidized perhaps the most remarkably successful system of adult education in the world—the Folk High Schools, where a term with all accommodations costs about 200 *kroner*, or perhaps nothing to a student subsidized by his local council—yet a government that puts no restriction on the pleasures of a gay and tenaciously pleasure-loving people, one of whose endearing small charms is to welcome, sincerely, with real and unrapacious interest, the foreigner.

SWEDEN

II

SWEDEN

THE master-key to the Swede is the sun.

There are several lesser locks to be negotiated; for with his Baltic soul and his era of seventeenth-century power and his exclusion from the last two large wars—and in addition his comparative wealth—he is one of the most complicated Europeans to evaluate. But it is still the sun that turns him deepest: both with its absence during the long dark winter months, when resignation can sink to melancholy, and with its sudden marvellous blaze of strength in spring and golden summer.

On the first warm day of spring the citizens of Stockholm, a busy enough city, may be seen sitting in their hundreds on the steps of the Dramatic Theatre or of the Concert Hall, their faces upturned towards the sun, their eyes closed, motionless, rapt. The first blossoming of buds, which is anywhere a pleasure, becomes an obsessional joy with the Swede. Normally a quiet, grave people who tend to smile rather than laugh, this annual awakening from the condemned chrysalis is truly passionate and not easy for our more temperate hearts fully to understand. There is a certain splendour in such excitement, one is reminded of the exaggerated pulsing of green blood in a fast-motion film of plant life; and one is reminded that all passion must be paid for. One suspects, too, that this split personality of the weather

43

is reflected in the general character of the Swede—somewhere beneath that kindly, pensive, ordered gravity, somewhere beneath his well-pressed cloth of sober grey, there burns a ball of fire yearning to explode. At times it does, and the literary cliché of the Big Crazy Swede comes alive—sunshine, art, jazz, or a pair of skis can kindle this smouldering yule; and of course, in a people largely concerned with ice and long darkness, it flares prettily on alcohol.

However, that is the eruption; but in terms of every day the Swedish character is far nearer the ball-bearing than the ball of fire—it is indeed as elegant, as polished, as refinedly functional as those fine spheric arrangements their industry has so efficiently perfected. Elegance is most noticeable in this country, elegance in craftsmanship such as glass and pewterware, elegance in a formality of manners largely uninvaded by modern laxity: but here again, though this might be a legacy of the great days of Gustavus Adolphus and Charles XII, we may be back with the sun-motif—for love of the sun has given the Swede a consuming love of nature, he is unhappy without a tree and a plant and a mossy stone within reach, Linnaeus lives on in his heart, and it may well be that a sensitive colloquy with the natural beauties engenders a wider elegance. By chance the word for Swedish is SVENSK, a rapier word that has a slender steel nicety about it compared with DANSK as broad as a Dane and NORSK as northern-bluff as a Norwegian. Fortuitously too the Swedish flag is blue and yellow, colours of sun and sunlit sky.

44

It is the countryside, then, that is more important to the Swede than his modern and functional city: and there are many sides to this countryside, for Sweden is a long country running north and south through several distinct kinds of latitude. Down in the south near Denmark the land is flat and flowering, the rape flower blazes its mustard colour across the fields, and there is corn and thatch. Nearly a thousand miles north harsh mountains of iron rise, ice-bound for most of the year, and in summer magical and desolate beneath the all-night sun. In between, with its vast fir forests and its ninety-six thousand lakes, the country extends a gradual compromise between these different poles. So—where to begin? Perhaps at the axis of compromise, at about the centre, at the part which is often called 'the heart of Sweden', the province of Dalarna known abroad as Dalecarlia.

It is in Dalecarlia, in the villages of the lovely and long lake Siljan, that old-fashioned peasant costume and handcrafts survive more than elsewhere in the country. The usual picture of the broad-hatted knee-breeched farmer, and of his wife in her striped apron and bodice, will more than likely come from here; and on Siljan the fiddlers still gather and the long church-boats strike out on the lake. These unusual craft, carrying fifty to a hundred villagers, garlanded with green birch leaves and rowed along their great length by many white-shirted menfolk, were once the ordinary means of visiting the several white churches that lie down by the water. With the building of proper roads they are now used only on more ceremonial occasions—and there is a unique boat-race between villages in the first week of July. Nevertheless, many of the people still continue to wear on Sundays the old costume, and though it may sound tourist-inspired and a little too near the living chocolate box to speak of a Dalecarlian walking through a white birch-alley in yellow breeches with scarlet pom-poms, and his lady in one of her dozen different formal costumes, whose patterns differ for funerals, weddings, Christmas and other festival occasions—though this sounds overcoloured it is not so: for these people will be at their ease, smoking a cigarette, calling a dog, exchanging diurnalities of crop or forest, and in a few seconds the distinction of costume is forgotten: the effect is not at all that of an actor in antiquated costume who has learned false gestures from posed prints and never lets you forget it—here it is an everyday matter, it is real and that is that.

A sight always more startling than a pair of daffodil breeches is the insistence of the white birch-tree. This lovely eccentric, with its slender branches that form so exquisite a filigree of silver in the hoar-frost, of misted green in spring, strikes hard as the white lines in a zebra hide against its dark consort of pine and spruce: erect and slim the birch, and one feels someone has gone mad with a whitewash brush among the trees, slashing the dark forest with brilliant streaks of white. Intensely white in the clear air, the bark looks painted or bandaged, and such is the effect of so many exact upward rising poles, dark spruce and white birch, with all their upper branches weaving to the sky, that suddenly the land

feels like the bottom of a sea and these trees a deli-
cately tressed marine growth stretching up into a
clear blue water which is for us the sky. Sometimes
the birches are planted formally to lead to a white
church, or to grove the avenues of a small town : but
more grow wild in the forests that stretch, for mile
upon monotonous mile, wide and far up and down
the land, a vast melancholy of trees for which the
Swedes feel intensely, as for a great and tender
music touched with sadness but as long and lonely
and lovely as life itself.

The Dalecarlians preserve their old customs as
they have preserved a historical independence of
character. Originally pocketed far away from the
seats of government, cut off by forests from all cen-
tralized power, they have remained freemen in
spirit—and even preserve studied differences from
village to village. Discussing the local fiddle-music, a
villager of Rättvik told me that their songs are much
sadder than those of Leksand, whose people are considered round-faced and southern : yet the distance
south is no more than a dozen kilometres . . . and
the people of Mora, fifty kilometres across the lake,
speak a dialect pagan-sounding and still harsh, they
say, with the blood of human sacrifice. Likewise the
handcrafts—one village specializes in knife-making ;
another carves the orange-vermilion little wooden
horses that are so prevalent an adornment of Swedish chimneypieces (alas, these are also now factory-
made near Stockholm, as are Lapp trophies) ; and
another village beats copper or iron. The painter
Anders Zorn lived at Mora, and many of his paint-
ings show the nineteenth-century villagers dancing

round the may-pole on Midsummer Eve just as they do to-day. (May deriving not from May but from an old word meaning to deck with leaves.)

But architecturally Dalecarlia has lost much of its spirit: the carved and painted wood porches are no longer contrived, and even the use of the traditional red Falu paint is declining. This pigment is still ubiquitous in Sweden: it is of a purplish red, an ox-blood colour, derived from by-products of the great old copper mine at Falun, and throughout the land the square, wooden, pitch-roofed houses are painted with it, their windows and cornices outlined in white —and well does this bright deep red marry with the dark green of spruce and pine. However—pale grey concrete is creeping in: perhaps not yet too obtrusively in a country so rich in timber, yet enough to upset the old homogeneity. A native simplicity of line hitherto softened by colour looks pretty dull. It becomes a pleasure to rest the eye on the loudly pretty, on say the florescent eaves of a nineteenth-century villa, when you can find one. Although the lines of the traditional wooden cottages were always simple, one could in the past and can sometimes now be confronted with a red house set in a field of yellow flowers with violets covering its old turfed roof and a white goat tethered aloft to a chimney to crop the turf, all quite possibly under a day-moon turned apple-green by the strange northern sunlight. Too much? But divested of similar softening features of colour and weather, functionalism taken to the Swedish degree cannot but be tedious and dispiriting.

Falun is the provincial capital of Dalarna, and is most celebrated for its huge old copper-mine, the

Lake Mälaren's ending in the centre of Stockholm

The oldest part of the Göta Canal

Trotting at Åby

Stora Kopparbergs Bergslags A.B., the oldest industrial concern in the world (deriving its licence from 1347). Its older workings now present a gigantic, dramatic gash in the earth surmounted by several pleasant old office-buildings. At one period of its history the output was so abundant that the government, to maintain European copper prices, decreed the minting of giant copper coins of great and awkward weight; people were forced to carry their money in sacks over the shoulder, and the rich to transport it by sleigh—an indisposition weightier than the original concern, and which was soon discontinued.

The small fields of Dalarna are studded with odd-looking hay-drying racks of weathered grey wood that stand stacked and slanting like Bofors guns—it is said that German air reconnaissance over such fields reported Sweden to be the best-defended country in Europe. This patchwork divisioning represents very small holdings, most being coupled with a portion of forest for timber production. The forest is always predominant. And it is the forest—laced with good motor high-ways along which the orange buses course, sliced by railroads speeding efficient electric-driven trains—which absorbs the traveller, along with a few elks and bears and wolves. The forest goes on for mile upon mile upon mile. It opens out into a lake, closes remorselessly again. By the shore of the lake there will have been time to see a golden flash of stacked pine-logs, and perhaps a single pink factory chimney that seems to float at the water's edge like the tall funnel of a river-boat. Then again the forest. And a river opens, and down it a match-stick jumble of logs drifts and hurdles, part of the immense timber production logging its way on the melted snows to key mills by the sea. Occasionally a church gleams white, its spire thin on a leekish onion of dark grey; and then a small town spreads itself as the trees fall away—yellow street signs, box-like houses, box-like flats, pale-grey or blood-red, orderly but unfenced, so that the feeling is of a very new, polished town put down yesterday and not quite finished: evidences of history, whether a fin-de-siècle villa or older warehouses or burghers' dwellings, are usually drowned by the later building. And on into more forest, making the flash of plate-glass windows and modern shops seem like a mirage only imagined; and now, until the next town or sawmill or isolated factory, there is only an occasional red farmhouse with its white-lidded black eyes, an unfenced unweathered toy put down for a moment in the wide green prospect—though it might have been there for two or three hundred years.

Suddenly a smelting works, for iron-veins are about under the green—and miraculously into the sky plumes a vivid orange smoke, rich and oriental. And in closes the forest again. In spring you may come across sudden carpets of oversize bluebells, in summer the sudden corn-fields strike a fine soft green against the forest dark—and in case the monotony of the forest has here been overstressed, it must be repeated that the trees are often white, there is in this and the red wood houses a construction of colour that invigorates. And everything is seen through the splendidly clear northern air, as enlivening to the eye as to the lung; but tiring to the feet—things look nearer than they are in such intense purity, a church that seems ten minutes away will take you twenty to walk to.

Meanwhile, as the forest green passes, as the pole-like trees dizzy as railings blur into miles, a glance at a paper or a scrap of conversation will be building up the feeling that this is Sweden, that these thousands of trees are *Swedish* trees and none other . . . a hundred odd observations, a hundred small remembered details will colour the trees with Swedish association . . . the fields of giant Dalarna bluebells, the enormous newspaper with its pages devoted to photographs of eminent townsfolk celebrating their birthdays, and other names shrouded with a heavy Lutheran cross to mark their deathday . . . and the charming measure of an old dance, the Hambo, lilting and momentarily wistful, danced still as we might occasionally dance a polka, though the Hambo is older . . . and a glass of hot Christmas *glögg*, made from *snaps* and steaming spiced wine . . . and the charming everyday use of French words transmuted into Swedish spelling, *buljong* for *bouillon*, *adjö* for *adieu*, and the onomatopoeic '*gonggong*' for our simple, lonely 'gong'. . . and pictures of June skiers, white-hooded, in Lapland . . . and a fierce-looking football result—Råå versus Höganäs . . . and the exotic idea of a country living on green gold and white coal . . . and the memory of a single Swedish chimneypiece decorated for Easter and offering, as well as the perennial assortment of brasses and red Dalarna horses and ceramic peasant figures and iron candelabra and potted creeper and ferns and woven cloth runners, a brilliant new influx of coloured chicken-feathers hung on birch twigs and coloured chickens' eggs and coloured wool chicklets and a whole amazing assortment of birds confected from matchsticks and red, blue, green, yellow bark and, superlative among these prettinesses, the first pale meagre bunches of beloved spring flowers.

From this central node of Dalarna, which may be thought of as a sudden patch of brightly coloured folk-weave material set in larger sobrieties rolling on to north and south, the ascent of the Swedish ladder brings always wilder and more remote land, up to and over the polar circle, where the iron-mountains rise and the Lapp people drive their reindeer herds: the opposite direction, the descent, encounters the capital and the district of great lakes and their Göta canal which cuts right across the country from Skagerrak to Baltic, a country of great old castles and great new industrial towns (quiet and clean, since the word 'industrial' connotes noise and smoke), until the flat south itself, the granary and the orchard.

Up in Lapland it is wild. A sick Lapp woman who arrived in the town of Jokkmokk expressed a fine eighteenth-century horror at the sight of a railway engine. This curious machine was explained to her. Then, as an afterthought, she was asked:

'How then did *you* get here?'

'How do you think?' was the answer. 'By plane, of course.'

This illustrates well the growing importance of a technological web that, modern but silver-thin, weaves over the vast untracked distances in the north. But the south is of course quite different, tracked and populated and grained with history . . . and yet, in between cities, to either side of roads, there is still a greater feeling of virgin country than in the body of Europe. The cities do not straggle with suburbs. You are out of them and by a lake or in woodland in a few minutes.

But leaving aside for a moment Stockholm—and also the northern territories which can be reached by aeroplane in a couple of hours from Stockholm—let us enter the prevalence of waters that ranges across the country between the capital and the second city and western port of Gothenburg (Göteborg). One of the most idyllic journeys in Europe must be the leisurely trip, through fields and over hills, in one of the tubby white steamers that ply between these two key cities along the lakes, rivers and canals: idyllic— but ghostly too, for it is strange and phantasmal to see across the meadows at noon on a summer's day a white ship rounding an edge of dark trees to come sailing through flowers and corn, noiseless and with the slow insistent movement of ships, the canal water invisible, a panic sight at the panic hour.

The journey dawdles into three days. You leave Gothenburg at nine in the morning of the first and arrive at seven in the evening of the third day at Stockholm. The steamer will have covered 347 miles of water, two-thirds of which is natural lake and river, the rest canal. It is a good, drowsy way of seeing the summer country. The ship is a moving pavilion under whose white canopy you can sit at ease and see pass, at a speed proper for ruminative digestion, the castle or the lakeland, the patient ore-barge or the red farmstead. You will sail up and over hills, and through mysterious tunnels of fir, over lakes wide and beautiful or deep and mysterious, past huge modern power stations or under such charming eccentricities as an old iron bascule bridge which, set against the leaves of an industrial village of the early nineteenth century, has all the still set tranquillity of an early steel engraving, of that peaceful marriage of iron and green that so entrances the atmosphere of all disused rail-stations and grass-grown canal-works.

The beginning is at Lilabommen Quay, opposite Frihamnen (The Free Port) in Gothenburg. The first hours take you up the broad reed-edged Göta river, past the battered grey bastions of the mediaeval fortress of Bohus, and on between cliffs to the first lock and to the power stations at Trollhättan. The first lake is Sweden's largest, Lake Vänern. This immense stretch of water still echoes the time, long before the Stone Age of man, when it was part of the ocean—a feeling of the sea persists in the lonely tinning of a bell-buoy, the cries of gulls, a steamer's smoke on the horizon, and possibly quite rough weather. Läckö Castle, a white baroque eminence with square towers and slate steeples, stands on an island promontory overlooking the broad waters—one of the many castles that stud the land all the way to the south. The Västgöta canal, opened as early as 1822, connects Vänern with the next large lake Vättern—and this part, with its old towpath and its winding way among trees and across small lakes, is the sleepiest, the most pleasantly seedy, of the journey. Across Lake Vättern lies, or rises like a mirage, the town of Vadstena, with its Castle and its Red Tower and its Blue Church, a trident silhouette: from the schoonered harbour you may go ashore and see the town, a quiet place whose streets still follow fifteenth-century directions and whose fine enmoated castle with its fat round bastions was built in 1552 by Gustavus Vasa, liberator of the Swedes from Danish suzerainty. But at other points, too, one can land and complement the armchair ease of the deck (and the steamer's throb) with a walk on firm land: particularly when the stair cases of locks have to be navigated—as at Berg further on, where a dramatic succession of fifteen locks lowers the craft to the level of Lake Roxen.

Such an account as this goes too fast, with too erratic a seizure on isolated objects, for what is in essence so leisurely a journey. Perhaps it is never the castle or the enterprise of lock-works that finally engages the memory: perhaps it is more simply that single cyclist on the tow-path, student cap white in the sun, whose bowed vanishing back describes a whole summer's day; or the sudden blond-maned horse above a hedge munching in a single moment what will be hours in your future memory. The mind wanders not at will but for a hundred more complicated reasons: and as one drifts through the meadows or along the fir-bound lakeside, it is possibly only the eye that glosses the green and lulling scene— the errant mind is back in Gothenburg, wincing again on the Giant Racer in Liseberg amusement gardens, or sitting in one of the city's parks, lilac-bound, with the blue and silver trams coursing like modern caterpillars across bridges over water that reminds the grass of its maritime heritage. It is intriguing to consider that this great port with its canal-set greenery was built by Dutch engineers; and that the Scots then developed much of it and that the eighteenth-century Bachelors' Club and such words as Avenyen (the Avenue) and family names like Carnegie and Campbell all persist in a Swedish port nicknamed Little London that had better be called Little Edinburgh.

Every great city has so many different aspects; and with Gothenburg one may first be impressed by the entrance into the harbour, with grey-black granite cliffs piling like a dead school of whales, a firm reminder that after the long reaches of Atlantic and North Sea hard land has been reached; and by a sky-mad mass of red-lead derricks and cranes that, seen through clear and smokeless air by the light of a lowcast morning sun, claws at the clouds like an aerial swarm of giant pink crayfish: or one may feel for the older town, with its eighteenth-century quays and its Dutch canals (most of which are now filled in, though a kind of ghost of them persists in the reflection of those remaining) and a few great buildings like the old offices of the East India Company, and the open-air market of flowers: or one may sense the lovely layout of park along the old moat where the town walls once stood, broad water and green to mark a maritime garden city: or—and this may be strongest—the feeling of well-planned space about the broad avenues and the tall blocks of bal-

conied flats set back to avoid all chasmal pressures
and the new towers of more flats rising on the higher
ground around, hundreds of squares of units of living
glittering their glass windows to the sun, the air, the
tops of trees—never the smoke: and then admiration
is demanded for Götaplatsen, a spacious square on
elevated ground where theatre, concert hall, art
museum and the most modern Scandinavian hotel
(also a work of art) converge round Milles's Poseidon
fountain—Götaplatsen is a most impressive forum of
the arts, surmounting the main avenue and, floodlit
at night, appearing like a giant theatre in itself.

So the Gothenburgers stroll about their pleasant
city—they are said to be different from other Swedes,
more easy-going like the southern people of Skåne,
and certainly they cross the roads noticeably slowly,
with an independent scorn of the wheeled beetle
after them. But do they laugh? Seldom in a restaurant do you hear a burst of laughter from a table:
seldom in the streets is there more than a smile; one is
told of the old street-wit peculiar to the workers, but
that too is gone. What, one wonders of a port of this
size—what do the visiting sailors, tuned to the
moving musics of Antwerp or Copenhagen, find to
do? There is a fine summer amusement park, and
one big dance-hall—but apart from these a landfall here must reflect something of the granite tone
of Gothenburg's cool ice-age cliffs.

Boating about Bohuslän, the grey and red granite
coast of skerries that courses up to the Norwegian
border, is another Gothenburger joy. You can be in
or on the sea within twenty minutes of the centre.
And this barren sea-coast with its peppering of

hump-backed rocks and its small yachting towns like Marstrand attracts the summering Swede from all over the country : that is, if he is not adoring the sun in Lapland, or enjoying the sandier beaches to the south towards Lund and Malmö—or painting a thousand miles off in the Balearic island of Ibiza, where an easelbound, bearded, sunglazed Swede may be found round every white street corner.

But we are not in Ibiza, nor Marstrand—we are still pumping up the green Göta canal on those leisurely three days to Stockholm; and by now threading our white ship between meadowed cows to the sleepy old spa of Söderköping. Though involved with small manufactures to the measure of its three thousand inhabitants, and though it is the repair station of the Canal Company, Söderköping (South Market) has that attractively quiescent atmosphere of all those places which were once great ports and have now retreated inland : in the Middle Ages it was a commercial junction as thriving as Stockholm—but the river slowly silted up, its maritime nature declined, grasses grew where men had worked, the Hanseatic merchants from Lübeck or Visby directed their intercourses elsewhere and one more great city of spires and monasteries and guild-halls faded to a swollen village : not much more than two churches (one with a fine example of the old Swedish separate wooden bell tower) and the ruins of a hospital remain—but the atmosphere is thick.

Three miles further on salt water begins with the bay of Slätbaken, and now the ship continues towards the true Baltic spray, horizons, salt-sea islands. A country has been crossed; the Baltic waters this side saw the ancient highly disciplined Viking ships that set off from Roslagen further north to give their name *ros* to Russia, while other Vikings above Bohuslän on the western side were beaching their long-boats on the shores of what was to be called America.

But the present sea-trip is a short one. The air of gull and lighthouse soon thickens into a wooded archipelago, and Södertälje embraces us with bay, harbour and the last stretch of canal into Stockholm's lake Mälaren. Mälaren is Sweden's third biggest lake. In fact, it is more land than water, so profuse are its spruce-dark islands. And now through these the little white boat weaves its way up to the first signs of Stockholm, a scattering of summer-huts, then the first suburban villas, finally the outcrop of big apartment blocks—all gradually freckling with the prescience of a great city these gentle fir-studded waters.

Then, quite suddenly, you are there.

Spires have risen round you, the traffic swirls thick, and the steamer is tying up at a very central place opposite a broad quay on which stands a column like the column of St. Mark in Venice. Behind rises a red-towered palace reminiscent of the Venetian campanile—Östberg's famous City Hall of Stockholm, a sly comment on the loose old soubriquet 'Venice of the North' but beautiful in its own right.

The City Hall is a fitting symbol, in some ways, of Stockholm itself. Let us not so much marvel that here is a building of the 1920s that has achieved an integrated beauty, but that so many different styles have converged successfully: for this graceful artifact of deep red brick with its green copper turreting and its golden crown-work is like a *chinoiserie* on a Venetian theme contrived by a Goth who has dreamed Bakstian fantasies—and yet has woken fresh with the ability to refine his fantasy with subtle entasis and good Greek moderation. Stockholm, which one may well imagine to be a grey if modern and graceful city of the north, is full of such careful exoticisms. 'Lion-gold' is a traditional colour that blazes across large stretches of eighteenth-century plaster; Falu red may cover a tall gabled house in the Old Town or equally a great apartment block isolated on its peripheral height; there are domes of violent green copper, there are oriental motifs in some of the new carved granite buildings, and high above the white ships of the harbour hangs a suspended restaurant shaped like its name, The Gondola. But these are the eccentric spangles that shine out in a city that must mostly be remembered for its wide and lucent stretches of water, its white ships, its clear glassy air, its green furring of landscape garden, its outspan of communal rectangular sky-buildings and its inspan of involved, vortical traffic.

Stockholm is a deep-water port for big ships of the Baltic; it is the administrative centre of a long land predominantly living off the timber of forests, iron deposits, and what can be manufactured from these with the help of snow-fed rivers and hydro-electric works providing the 'white coal' of an almost coalless land; it has a million inhabitants, a seventh of the entire Swedish population, and the reputation among provincials of being busy, hard-hearted, impersonal—the reputation of every other capital city from London the Great Wen to that residence of the Devil, Dublin.

Unlike most other capital cities, it is not gay. It is beautiful, it offers exquisite food and fine theatre and other metropolitan pleasures, and at night it is bright-lit. Restaurants are luxurious and hushed, with sometimes a pianist playing light, palm-lounge music: you may even be refused entry on suspicion of being drunk if you approach with too much of a laugh and a swing. There are big popular dance-halls, like the National, where youth has its more animated fling; and in some restaurants there is dancing of a smooth evening-dress nature. The summer provides an amusement park on the Djurgården island at Skansen—and then, as always with the sun and the open air cafés, there is more liveliness. But generally the Swedes take it gently, courteously, quietly. At home, in a private party, there is gaiety: the Swede is a generous host, and once across the threshold anything can happen. But in public it is generally otherwise—apart, as ever in these northern places, from the liquor cases.

For years, until its moderation in October 1955, Sweden lived under the shadow—or some may say in the calm enlivening glow—of the Bratt system of liquor rationing. Hard liquor for hip or home could only be bought from State Monopoly shops on a ration card (based on 3 litres a month for adults); in restaurants food had to be eaten with alcohol and even then the consumption was severely limited, with half-measures for ladies. The cheap plate of hash obligatory with a drink was seldom really consumed, being brought out again and again for new customers : but this kind of atmosphere, and the watchful eye of the waiter, hardly engendered a wonderful conviviality; light wines were fairly free, but expensive in a land without vines, and beer was very 'near', about 2 per cent alcohol. That is all over now. But it is probably this, rather than the Swedish temperament, which has kept the city habitually so quiet. Yet one cannot be certain; for the Swede is difficult to predict—with his stiff traditional manners but his delight in modern design and material innovation, or with his puritan air but his almost renowned sexual ease (about 10 per cent of all Swedish children are illegitimate, and that is only part of the story). Where this comparative sexual freedom derives from is difficult to say: it is a general Scandinavian, even nordic tendency. It may be part of the climate of social progress—part of the throwing off of restriction, of planning for comfort and equality (including sexual equality, which reduces the woman's defensive instinct). Paradoxically again, in a country given much to benign bureacratic restriction, there is a straightforward lack of prudery: and certain it is that unmarried mothers are well looked after, without at least official opprobrium. No nonsense, too, in a country of otherwise such formal manners, about near-nakedness on the beaches: the nordic love of fine physique, together with sun worship, sees to this. One notices, too, a lack of restriction of magazines of erotic photographs, either designed with a body-beautiful-and-sane surface appeal or openly excitative: these decorate every tobacconist's window, and contrast curiously with the air of grave ordered decency which marks the rest of the street.

Together with her equality in most matters, the Swedish woman has still to contend with one drawback—the amount of her. Her superiority in numbers makes for a superiority of attitude in the male. He can, to put it brutally, too easily pick and choose: the sexual situation is deflationary, too few men chasing too many women. 'The Orient begins at Malmö,' it has been said, with reference to these despotic, sultanly tendencies. Yet—this question of numbers, which in any case occurs elsewhere, may be a simplification. Other factors are present. For instance, the Swedish industrial revolution came late, it is possible that the rural pattern of farm-master and house-woman dies hard, persists not too unconsciously: and it is precisely this that the emancipated lady will kick against—with both attitudes, tyranny and revolt, in this case working to one end.

It may be suggested that life in Stockholm, with its good eating, its café-and-cream-cake interstices, its good music and theatre and art, its accessible nature-life for riding or boating or swimming or ski-ing—that this is enough, that greater effusion is unnecessary. Yet one wonders: and one feels an air not of simple enjoyment but of light tension, of some kind of spiritual dissatisfaction. Industrious, perfectionist, the Swede works hard and pays high taxes and enjoys for this a high standard of living fairly distributed. Poverty is nil. It is a welfare state that has progressed far. But it may be that the achievement of such a physically sound position, with its emphasis on the reasonable middle way and its implicit condemnation of excess and eccentricity, leaves the bewildering question: What For? Old philosophical arguments erect their pesky heads. He who wins, loses. Achievement is no end, arrival no more than a further point of departure. But in any case, no one would wish the situation retracted and the cruelty of the old stews returned. Perhaps, after all, and in terms of temperament, we are back with the sun again—and with a discontent more divine.

The shortest river in the world, the Ström, runs at the centre of Stockholm. The Ström is the few hundred yards of controlled water connecting Lake Mälaren with the Salt Sea. To its west lie the fresh water islands and their pale cliffs of apartment houses, Chicagoesque; and to the east the beginning of the huge labyrinthine salt water archipelago leading to the Baltic, with islands silhouetting the Grand Hotel and the National Museum, the red castles and the red-lead ships' turrets of a naval base, the docks, and the extensive wild parkland called Djurgården. To grasp Stockholm's shape it may be easiest to imagine an hour-glass of water resting on its side, with the main city lying in its curves, and at the confluential narrowing of the glass a neck of island which constitutes the Old Town, the old fortified hub—now a fine hubbub of narrow streets and tall seventeenth-century mansions and cellar shops and taverns, with the great square Royal Palace massive and commanding at one end, indeed more than any

Manorhouse in Värmland

Storm beneath the Swedish calm—von Rosen's *Sfinxen* (National Museum)

Leksand church boat on Lake Siljan

Abstract play sculpture for children in a Stockholm park

other Royal Palace a centrifugal point, a presence which, crossing and recrossing the city, one never seems to avoid.

But one would not wish to avoid it. A square baroque hunk designed by Tessin, it is properly commanding, its lines are suavely clear, and the immense golden-tan walls, and the many windows of some of its five hundred or so rooms survey much of the King's business—waters and ships, the spires of churches and the cornices of Parliament: and also—and one senses a royal shrug from the royal apartments—the inquisitive windows of the Grand Hotel facing the Palace across the water.

Further up from the Grand Hotel is moored a three-master sailing ship, white and resplendent, one of Stockholm's outstanding watermarks. It is a youth hostel, and here a member of the organization can have a bed for a crown or two against umpteen for a good room at the Grand, yet with nearly the same binocular trajectory on the Palace. The youth hostel system is widespread throughout Sweden, anyone can join irrespective of age and means, and it is said—probably partly truly—that nowadays the average guest drives up in his own automobile. Meanwhile a less widely spread youth problem invests contemporary Stockholm—in too considerable numbers the dressed up corner-boys conglomerate in main squares to cause any empty-headed trouble that strikes them, to break up things, and occasionally to bring out the police—who still wear sabres, and at difficult moments use the flat; it seems that a noncombatant nation feels the spiritual post-war vacuum as much as—or more than?—the involved combatant. By this it is

not suggested that generally Sweden's youth is un-
cared for, for it is much the opposite; but only that
the big-city problem exists, grows, and finds no immediate solution.

The Old Town, with its high decorated gables,
its lanterns and its alleys, is not unlike Dutch or
North German agglomerations of similar date. But
here it is beautifully contained on the one small
island and is thus able to keep itself to itself without
modern intrusion. And on closer acquaintance it
could never be German, you are constantly reminded
of its truly Scandinavian nature—by such as the
dragon engaging St. George's interest in the Storkyr-
kan (The Great Church), for this dragon has elk's
antlers; and as always by street-names and signs
blazoning the language, the indelible message of a
Viking land and nowhere else—Gåsgränd, Skeppar
Olof, Västerlånggatan. In the cellar restaurant
called The Golden Peace (Den Gyldene Freden), a
place of old stone walls and copper pans, the poet
Bellman's songs are still sung to the lute; and the
copper pans are still made round the corner in the
little square called Tyska Brunnsplan. It is a romantic old place at any time of the year; but perhaps it
is seen best of all in snow, with the cold white fleec-
ing its warm reds and pinks and yellows and greys,
when the cellar-shops shine snugly and the narrow
streets cut off the wind, a life-size Christmas card
with the iron of truth in it.

The Old Town stands separate. It is like an excur-
sion town within the wider city that towers south on
the great rock Södermalm, or fans out on the flatter
north rock where the theatre and bright-light dis-

trict lies. Södermalm is largely the working class quarter, it is reached either by the rising whirl of traffic fly-overs at Slussen, an architecture in itself; or by the exposed Katarina Lift which for a few *öre* raises the pedestrian far above the city to blench from or delight in the vast, at last comprehensible map extending below. Now the lie of these involved waters becomes plain—you can see the parklike Djurgården island to the east, with its marvellous open-air Skansen museum of all the old village architectures of the country, with its wild riding woods and its leisurely villa-palaces built for an ampler age, and also what must be the most spacious studio a private painter has ever attained, the enormous royal paintery at Waldermarsudde of fin-de-siècle Prince Eugen, friend of Zorn and devotee on a truly royal scale of his art. Just past the King's Palace rises the mournful iron spire of Riddarholm Church, where seventeen Swedish monarchs lie buried; beneath it the lovely rose and grey music of pilaster and pediment called Riddarhuset, the House of Knights, another jewel of this restrained northern baroque; and beyond, and if you stand here at dusk, extend the exceptionally clear-glowing green and red neon lights of Stockholm delineating their radiation of theatre and shopping streets against a unique clarity of blue, of intensely cold clear electric blue twilight. All around, on gentle hills across water, the regular rectangular apartment lights glitter like orderly machines, like illuminated telephone switchboards; one group in tall units with pitched snow-roofs looks like a range of giant sail-less windmills : and over on Södermalm there ranges the mass of lights marking

Södersjukhuset, a hospital so large that the nurses sometimes have to cycle between wards; beyond— the graceful Västerbron bridge throws its necklace on the waters, on the night.

From up on the Katarina Lift Stockholm looks a dazzling vibrant city, a Paris of a place. But descend into the streets at some time after eleven at night, and outside the peak summer months—and one is perplexed by a certain emptiness in the streets. All the lights blazing—but oddly few people about. They hardly seem to be the streets of the same city one saw from the bridge, nor indeed of the capital of a rich country. There is a feeling of vast crowds behind doors, that in a minute a dozen theatres will open their doors and the people come milling out. But they do not. The lights shine on in an empty aquarium, on a place that is not exactly human— for whom are they on for? And Stockholm, which frowns on a late night life, calmly puts itself to bed. No night clubs. A few dispersed latish restaurants with dancing. A few bars that close soon after midnight. Nothing else.

But life by day, when those deceptive lights are off, is richer. Swedish food is excellent, more refined than elsewhere in Scandinavia, and great attention is paid to the look and colour of garnishings (a Swedish housewife arranging the little canapés of *smörgås-bord* before her party takes trouble and time that would horrify a less formal foreigner). Dinner is generally eaten as early as five-thirty or six o'clock, grading with the occasion up till eight. The habit of an organized aperitif hour has never taken on in Stockholm, there is nothing to delay the meal-hour.

Fine eating can be enjoyed in such modern restaurants as Riche or La Ronde, or at the Trianon set on its own little island, or between the more mellowed walls of the Opera Cellar (Operakällaren) and the 1,500-seater called Berns whose lavish chandeliers and gilded plush were suggested by the interiors of the Paris Opera, and one of whose private dining rooms is the original of Strindberg's *The Red Room*. *Smörgåsbord* is of course the hallowed prelude, and is well known to range its canapés from smoked reindeer to elk-balls and through the salmons and eels to a subtlety of herrings smoked or soused or sweet. Dishes of sustenance follow ordinary Parisian models —but such as roasted elk in a white cream sauce can be very good, and, if you can get it, *gravlax*, which is raw salmon treated with saltpetre to attain a jellied texture and the taste of a dream of smoked salmon purified even of its smoke. All can be preceded by a sting or two of aquavit, potato-based from the south, wood-based from further north, but in either case to be drunk ceremoniously with a grave nod and a long look straight in the eye before the little glass is lowered: I have noticed in Spain a similar ritual when a cigarette is given—both habits must have evolved from a kind of pipe-of-peace gesture— though with Swedish aquavit it sometimes looks like the stasis of a sudden shock produced by the strength of the alcohol itself, as if paralysis has set in below. In passing—wood-alcohol has no hooch-connotation here; it is quite safe in a timber country where even wood-steaks have been eaten in restaurants, acclaimed to be all right but not too wonderful, and now relegated to cattle-feeding.

And the extra-prandial pleasures? One of the little white steamers out to, say, Vaxholm, for the day—the Stockholmers say these old steamers know every rock on the archipelago, they've been on all of them . . . or a visit half-an-hour out to the royal palace of Drottningholm, a stately white beauty with a chinese rococo pavilion and uniquely an eighteenth-century theatre with all machinery still working, where plays are shown in the dress and according to the custom of the period . . . or to the Nordiska museum to see the fine collection of decorated sleighs . . . or to the National Museum to see the Rembrandts, Modiglianis, Watteaus and much else—and here of particular interest are the nineteenth-century pictures of painters like Zorn and Bergh, and the brilliant mad Josephson, all of whose scenes of Swedish life, with their strong atmospheric overtones of melancholy and of the timeless twilight of long summer evenings, enable one to understand a little better the Swedish temperament—and two much-used words, *längtan* (a vague longing) and *stämning* (something like a stirring of senses of time and place) whose incidence in a language of small vocabulary is significant; for ours so much richer can only produce 'nostalgia', and too often misuse it at that.

Or one might take the tram to the Haga Park, where the elegant art-loving Gustav III built an exquisite little palace and an exotic cavalry barracks in the form of immense copper-roofed tents . . . or wander in the flower market by the fine modern concert house and watch a street pedlar barking his wares—about the only mildly eccentric class left in Stockholm . . . or sit in a café and note that Swedes are not predominantly blond like the Norwegians, they are on the whole darkish-haired, though when they are blond they are startling so, hence the popular myth . . . and listen to the greetings, '*Hej, Hej,*' and the word of thanks '*tak tak*' tapping on all sides like a woodpecker gone mad on a typewriter . . . or drive through an early spring fog when the little parks and the lampstandards are wreathed with mist as in the background of an early UFA film . . . and notice there is something UFA about the ladies, something a little outmoded and Germanic in the coquetry of a hat, the formidable hang of a string of pearls : and do they perhaps move differently, their feet primping outwards, their stance a trifle *dramatisch*?

Or in winter go skating for miles among the Mälaren islands, a manual windsail saving your own breath (some people skate as far as Upsala, seventy-three kilometres away) . . . or ski anywhere in the surrounding hills, even as close in as Haga . . . or in summer take the 55-minute plane to the lovely island of Gotland and stay the night at Visby, a walled mediaeval town, old Hanseatic capital of this island of 'roses and ruins', of wild ponies and wilder orchids, an astonishing Baltic survival with nearly a hundred churches built before 1350. . . .

Or—and here again the Swedish paradox winks a bewildering eye—happen on one of the annual feast-days, such as the eighth day of August, when the open crayfish-eating season begins . . . and watch a recessive people break out. On this day of days the Stockholmers assemble in parties in their summer houses on the islands, or out in the open countryside, and set up tables under paper lanterns to gorge themselves beatifically on piles of the tasty little red monsters. Songs are sung, and much aquavit drunk. 'You are supposed to drink a glass for every claw you eat,' a giant big-boned face told me, 'and you eat a dozen, two dozen before the night is out—and so, if you aren't careful, are you.'

On Midsummer night, the lightest of the year, when in the north the sun never sets and on Stockholm's latitude the dark is scarcely worth worrying about—on this night called St. John's an ancient pagan ritual brings the dancers out, and the maypole is celebrated till the early hours: the tall staff covered with green leaves and decked with wreaths stands against a pale midnight sky with a certain priestly presence, most ancient emblem of things green that grow in the worshipped sun. But the dancers underneath have forgotten these origins, nowadays it is just a good excuse to make a night of it up in Dalarna's hills or round Stockholm or down in Skåne, throughout the length and breadth of the country—and the celebrant hearts are of course now Lutheran or part of other protestant nominations like *Filadelfia*: they have long forgotten what they are really doing, despite the fact that sun-worship and sun-craving are still so much part of their real and daily *Angst*. Walpurgis Night, the eve of the First of May, sees bonfires lit on hills everywhere, again a fiery orison to the coming green of summer: and no witch can stand it, they say—the wintry old hags are up on their broomsticks and far away by dawn. To celebrate the winter solstice in December there is the charming ceremony of Santa Lucia, when

72

girls dressed in white and crowned with lighted candles pay a ritual homage to the coming re-birth of the sun, and everyone puts a lighted orange-red star in his window. On Christmas Eve, still called in Sweden by the old seasonable word 'yule', special Christmas dishes of *lutfisk* and rice pudding are put outside to placate the yuletide gnomes; on Twelfth Night the saturnalia puts on a new dress with a group of boys dressed in white cloaks and white conical hats, one of them always masked and grotesque to represent Judas Escariot. It is axiomatic that pagan myth and pagan celebrations have everywhere been absorbed into the Christian calendar—but here, as with the churches where so often a sun motif is emblazoned above the altar, the ancient spirit seems always closer at hand: the forests and the long dark nights are powerfully present.

The sun returns us to the night-life of Stockholm —and one grave omission. For Stockholm does offer an unusual summer diversion—the flight to the midnight sun. The plane leaves in the evening between ten and eleven o'clock, by one o'clock in the morning the well-dined Stockholmer is circling above the great lakes and wild valleys of northern Lapland, a moth in the light of the low lantern sun; by four o'clock he is back home again in the capital. In that time, he will have passed up and down his entire long country, far above the spires of Upsala of the white-capped students, up and up over log-bearing rivers and forests and charcoal-burners' huts, over farms and villages of wooden houses, over forest-bound mouse-trap and cotton-reel factories, past Skellefteå whose iron deposits contain so much arsenic that this embarrassing by-product has to be sunk away in concrete vats, past Boliden where gold is mined, over bears and wolves and elks and deer and eagles and the great long-skirted owls of the north, up to the land where Lapps live encamped in hide and birch wigwams (*kåtor*) with their reindeer herds, up to the mining town of Kiruna which boasts the largest city area in the world (about five thousand square miles), up to where suddenly there might flash the long glass roofs of extraordinary settlements for forcing tomatoes and cucumbers and strawberries in the glaring months of strong sunlight—and finally to Lake Torne Träsk near the Norwegian border, a magic of flowering desolation in the light of a low-lying lambent night-loving sun.

The shadow of the passing aeroplane might mean two things to the Lapp beneath—it might remind him of his grey reindeer herd as it moves in winter like a shadow across the distant mountain snows, or he might think of the aeroplane itself and wonder whether a friend's fishing catch was aboard for the market, or a sick person for the hospital, or anything else that has made this most advanced form of transport the most reasonable one in emergency for this least mechanized of Sweden's people. Lapps live off their reindeer herds or by fishing among mountains and valleys without roads and with few tracks : their way of life has remained comparatively primitive—except for this occasional aeroplane, and one or two smaller machines, like the sewing machine that takes such pride of place in the conical tent, and the wireless, which, on my first visit to a Lapp tent in winter, lulled the violet snows with the warm-scented strains of *La Vie en Rose.*

As a pork-canner uses up in some way all of the pig, so a Lapp rationalizes his reindeer. Its strength is used for transport (pack or sleigh), its flesh for meat, its hide for clothing and for building, its fur for warmth, its horn for knives. Of an estimated ten thousand Swedish Lapps, about three or four thousand are nomadic: there are over twice as many across the Norwegian border, and several thousands in Finland and Russia. Though the number of breeders is declining the number of reindeer has increased—there are thought to be about two hundred thousand now in Sweden. Breeding them, following the herds on their moss-munching migrations down from the wolves in winter and up from the mosquitoes in summer, is an arduous though profitable life. It is no longer right to talk of the Lapps generally as a nomadic people, for they are beginning to prefer huts to tents, to form settled communities, to cultivate the land, and to fish. Although they speak different dialects, their *lingua franca* is an old form of Finnish: they still wear a decorated traditional costume, the woman in her apron and big skirt and lace cap, the man in a loose fitting blue and red coat and a cap topped with a huge red pompom, so that he looks rather like a miniature Italian *bersagliere* gone red on top. The nomadic Lapp children are served with nomadic schools in the summer; and although at heart his worship is still very close to nature—there are strange tales of telepathic powers over great distances and of an ability to hear 'music' from stones—he is properly a Christian, though he may be able to visit the church only twice a year, when accumulations of marriages and christenings are celebrated *en masse*, with dogs in attendance.

The land these strange, slit-eyed little people live in is surprisingly luxuriant in summer. Flowers grow to twice their normal size, the sun remains out all night—and the mosquito breeds in millions. Over the flowered wilderness one may see at midnight a nearly naked hiker glistening with anti-mosquito oil, headless in a white gauze hood, his pale midnight shadow stalking behind: one may see also the luxurious electric carriages of the Land Cruise train from Stockholm coursing like a reddish caterpillar through the rich, dwarfing desolation—an eight-day trainful of people, showers, restaurant, cinema, library, and bar humming along in comfort over the reindeer moss and heather, past snowcapped mountains and immensely calm lakes, over country softened by Atlantic warmths but really on a parallel with the centre of Greenland. Like all lonely unpopulated places, Lapland beggars description: the essence is in the sense of time and space that weighs the air, in the feeling of age and of permanence, so that three-score-years-and-ten truly seem, and somehow not unpleasantly, like the drop of a stone in the lake.

But in winter? Then life must feel like the drop of a stone on the ice of the lake—paused, frustrated, extended unendurably throughout dark hours unnaturally long. *Lappsjuk*, Lapp sickness, the Swedes call the languor of the northern mind in winter. And this is not only true of the extreme north, for the country is snowbound throughout its length. The Bothnian ports are frozen fast, you can drive a car over lakes frozen with ice a yard and more thick, the petrol-blue rivers of summer turn to bottle-green torrents snaking through bull-icicles big as organ-pipes, locomotives arrive hoary and ice-hung like the heavy black monsters met in nineteenth-century Russian novels: and indeed with high fur caps and greatcoats the whole of the mystery of ice and fur, snow and fire invigorates the cold white land. Because the Swede, and the visitor to his country, likes to think in terms of summer, this account has emphasized the golden months—but that is of course only a third of the story, the rest is snow and frost and the bravura of torchlit sleigh-rides under a blue velvet sky studded with stars of ice. Or, if you like, sitting by a rubber-plant in double-windowed steam-heat—for the Swedes are not like the damp English, they have made themselves comfortable. Even the reindeer's horns are covered with a warm, mossy fur.

And it does seem finally that this long dark winter, with its endless introspective hours—plus a comparative wealth for so northerly a nation—has given the Swede his aptitude as a perfectionist: as someone who, one notices, can flavour his envelope gum to taste sweet, wind up the end of his tooth-paste tube with a key, place a litter box marked 'Matches' outside a country school; and in larger matters is fair and socially progressive for the good of all, and is become peacable after having been, like the Swiss, one of the professionally ablest militarists of Europe.

FINLAND

Finnish forester

Helsinki harbourline, with the Great Church white above grey and rose pal

Modern church and belfry at Salla

III

FINLAND

FROM the Palace Guardhouse, rose-pink against the snow, a fur-capped company in pale grey greatcoats swings off easily past frozen harbour quays. Bright music played on curiously elongated French horns takes them up towards the kiosked, tree-lined Esplanade. They steam as they march. Each man carries a rifle whose butt is of polished walnut, like a piece of elegant furniture. Ducks pause to watch them from the apron of ice, fur-clad shoppers from the bright-windowed pavements. An enormous dark blue policeman holds up a skid of automobiles on the iced roadway, each chromium nose glitters to a miraculous safe standstill, and the little band passes and disappears in a dazzle of low golden sunlight, its distant music drowned in a breezy clatter of morning snow-shovels. . . .

Chinese lanterns burned orange against a sky of pale rich green, a brocade of a sky. It was ten o'clock in the evening, still warm. Warm outside as the sound of summer laughter and the drift of a concertina from boats on the gulf, warm inside as the vodka breathing its own fierce contentment. On each of our plates—we were sitting on the restaurant terrace—little red crayfish rose in piles both intricate and succulent: a pity to shatter such perfect little machines, but a sin of gastronomy to refrain. Suddenly, from nowhere, a little wind came: the gulf waters rippled, three or four becalmed white sails took a sudden step forward, each like the pointing of a dancer's toe, and the breath of a tremor trembled in the trees on the opposite shore: one, two seconds only—and it was all over, the calm again descended, and with it the smells of resin and salt warm air: the moment relaxed again into the strange, restive indolence of summered languor and high northern spirits that distinguishes this August city.

The onion bulbs of the old Orthodox cathedral were on the boil: it was fourteen below and steam from the warm air within gave this curious cauldron effect. No other movement round the harbour but the slow trudge of a squat black ice-breaker. When the harbour is frozen, it looks more than anything as if the tide has gone out. Whitish ice instead of mud: but the same shipwrecked effect. The islands look dead and stranded. Seabirds walk about pecking—but at what? A flotsam of occasional paper or a yellow crate waits to float again one day. Everything is dead, clutched in the winter grip. And then the sun comes out, the ice turns a golden rose, red spires on a promontory flash into being, the silt of dead ships and cranes comes to as lively a life as fills the snow-decked Christmas streets a minute's walk back in the town, streets festooned with brilliant light-bulbs and lulled with soft loudspeakered bell-music.

From the deck-chair looking up, it is the same planked canopy and the same old engine throb as in a river-boat steaming up the Congo or the Nile. But it is not so hot. It is freshly warm, and the lowered eye sees on the bank no swelter of mud and tropic palm but a clarity of spruce and a clean granite shore. There are naked bodies, though.

82

FINLAND

Occasionally one sees groups of the natives, naked but for a short towel or slip, sunning their bodies by the little bath-houses painted pale grey, or lichenous green, or dark red. The natives will have finished their office day at about four, thence to drive the half-hour out here to sweat themselves fresh in the hothouse and plunge into cool water—and now to relax in a sunlight that will continue yet for hours, to the clink of a glass of cold beer, or of the much-favoured gin and grape-fruit, or of a local cognac. And more and more spruce, more and more pine is passed as the old white steamer hammers on. Suddenly a steward's voice: '(Miss) Kyllikki Tapiovaara!' He repeats it, it echoes round the ship and against the dark bands of spruce. Where can she be, Miss Tapiovaara? And such a name—where on this earth can we be?

We are in or near Helsinki, the sea-bred capital of Finland. The above four purpling passages could each have begun a story placed in this one city at different times of year: in the cold but brisk and magic winter, in the warm three-month summer that can be counted as a five-monther, since most of the nights are days. As with New York and its extremes of cold and heat, you cannot paint Helsinki at once in both colours; it must be one or the other. Helsinki does not get as hot as New York, you could scarcely fry an egg on the pavement: yet in the *sauna*, the national dry steam bath, you do sit in air heated to 110° Celsius, so that an egg clasped in your hand would indeed obligingly boil. Miss Kyllikki Tapiovaara comes into the story only to brace the nerves with her name, with a couple of Finnish words, in anticipation of the full impact of this astounding language, oriental in origin, of treble vowels and double consonants, which the Finns engagingly boast can be spoken by only four million people in the world, themselves.

But before approaching Finland in proper detail, a non-political account such as this must first establish an important political condition. Finland is a democracy with all liberties intact. Each Finn is legitimately a free person, and in spirit a lot freer than some of his democratic brothers in other countries. It is often vaguely imagined that, because Finland borders on Russia, a shadow autocracy persists. Emphatically, this is not so : Finland is as freely conducted—and often on similar lines—as her Scandinavian neighbours. A Finn is a Finn is a Finn, as Madame Stein might have said, and that is that is that.

In external affairs, it is natural that the Finns wish for good relations with the colossus next door. Trade prospers, and good manners are observed. But this without obsequiousness—the Finnish Press (there are about a hundred and twenty newspapers; and Finland has the highest literacy in Europe) may freely criticize Russia or crack a joke at her expense. And for their part, the Russians have, for instance, made the gesture of handing back the Porkkala peninsula voluntarily. There remains in force a military pact that Finland will fight should Russia be attacked via Finnish territory: so there is no exact neutrality. But that is as far as it goes. The Finns rebutted Communism at the beginning, in the civil war of 1918, and have steered clear ever since. The

Finn communist party itself is small: it is strongest, oddly, up in the Lapp regions, but this is an indication perhaps of its idealist rather than pro-Russian nature. The well-known story of how Finland worked hard and paid up in full its onerous war reparation debt to Russia becomes more understandable: it was as much a demonstration of independence as of remarkable honesty. Finland had seen its brother country across the gulf, Estonia, accede to the Soviet. And Finland decided, firmly and painstakingly, to remain independent. So she went to work with a will, and paid up.

But it is an ill wind which blows no good—for since the Russians had to be paid in kind, and not only in the wooden kind of kind that constitutes the natural wealth of this country of great forests, new industries had to be created, industrialization took a pounce forward, and the national economy naturally remains the richer for this. A similar illish wind—the limitation by the Peace Treaty of Finland's army and other military resources—leaves her Budget free of the sort of armament bill that cripples most of us these days, and she can spend her money on wise and peaceful projects. (Similarly, a good wind also blows good: since the Olympic games of 1952, Helsinki has now a number of great modern hotels and a massive stadium of unique beauty, the legacy of special effort. That a wind should blow seems the desideratum: calm is the true enemy.)

Helsinki is a bracing little capital. Its centre rises round a salt-sea harbour open to the Baltic, and if one is so fortunate as to arrive by sea, then the first sight of classic palaces lining the quay, crowned above by the white majesty of the gold-and-green domed Great Church, flanked to one side by the involved brick and the onion domes of the Orthodox Cathedral, a fitfully exact tsarist touch—then this first sight will seem a mirage, a breathtaking prelude to no small Baltic capital but a city of great splendour.

And what, one may wonder, does a 'small' capital really mean in terms of the daily round? Not much. You can still get lost in it, walk your feet off in it, discover always something new round a corner; the glass in your hand is not smaller than elsewhere; the people who pass seem as infinitely various; and perversely in Helsinki, the restaurant you sit in will be a a lot larger than elsewhere, for the Finns like to eat in bulk among proportions of bulk. Nor does 'small' mean culturally small. The theatre is intensely alive, providing among much else even such delicatessen as a Finnish translation of *En attendant Godot*. The cabarets bristle with international artistes. Architectural and furniture design is of a world-reputedly high level. Orchestral music flourishes naturally in the country of old Sibelius. So what is small must be relegated to the minds of perhaps some élite social merry-go-round, or the figures of an economic gazette.

What is finally most interesting about a city is not the aggregate of its accomplishments, its beauties and its deficiencies—which the practical mind ticks off automatically, like an engine ticking over—but rather exactly *how* this particular city differs from

others; in qualities of atmosphere, in daily detail.
Thus with Helsinki one might add to the harbour
approach that there extends backwards the usual
tram-happy hub of shopping streets and offices; and
an official centre of classic building; and thence outwards suburbs made up mostly of large apartment
blocks; and that inlets from the Baltic occur everywhere to give the place a feeling of being built on
many islands among sheets of water. But these are
very bare bones. Let us rather pause to remember
that Helsinki lies on the Stockholm–St. Petersburg
line, that six hundred years of affiliation with Sweden
were passed before she became a Grand Duchy of
Russia in 1809, and that this more recent Russian
domination then lasted over a hundred years: and
that is why definitively I write St. Petersburg rather
than Leningrad, for it is the tsarist Russian touch
that strikes the romantic eye above what are otherwise Scandinavian qualities. The Orthodox Cathedral, with its gilded interior and its bubbling of
domes. The Orthodox cemetery, with little domes
among the graves. The high fur hats and fur coats
of the men in winter—many more than in Stockholm,
which seems consciously to have Americanized itself. The open-air markets in the country towns, the
women with their heads bound in kerchiefs and
swelling with skirts above felt boots. The Russian
piquancies of sour cream and caviare and blini and
gherkins that vary the usual Scandinavian kitchen.
Vodka rather than aquavit. And so on. Small touches
always appearing, and pleasing to the traveller bred
on the romance of Turgenev and Chekov.

The Finn will not be so pleased to hear this. Apart

from recent wars, tsarist Russia is remembered as an historical oppressor, and the feeling runs very roughly the same as the Irishman's towards England. Yet time and again I heard the present-day Russian spoken of amiably as a person : even so far, once, and in respectful confession, that the Russian can out-drink the Finn, which means a lot from a man who admires his own capacity. This general touchiness on the Russian flavour was nicely, and unconsciously, pointed to me one evening at dinner in Helsinki. My Finnish host spoke good English, as so many do, but had the usual difficulty in pronouncing 'sh', a compound uneasy on the Finnish tongue. The compromise sound was 'isis'—thus the word 'dishes' becomes 'disises'. So there was my proud and innocent Finn handing me a plate of blini and saying with marked generosity: 'One thing I will say. Finland has many delicious Russian diseases.'

One will notice, as slowly the character of the place becomes focussed, that drifts of white snow on coloured buildings have the same softening effect, but in negative, as soot shadows on the white stone of our more smoky cities . . . and how in summer there are so many children about—for from June to September is a three-month holiday from school . . . and how leisured and detailed is the ordering of food in a restaurant—the diner seems to be discussing some matter of impossible complication, the waitress's face is set in a matrix of wonder and concentration terrible to observe . . . and one will see how lavatories are designated by pictures not words, by

drawings of a man and a woman, a male hat and a
female bonnet—even so far as a cock pheasant and a
hen, a matter of possible embarrassment to the city-
bred visitor . . . and one will hear how in this
country, geo-politically placed as a first victim of a
future mondial war, they talk less of the possibility
of war than anywhere else, for the very impossi-
bility of doing anything about it has lifted both
responsibility and anxiety. . . . Though they still speak
about the last war more than elsewhere . . . when
one will hear how the Finns built their beloved
steam-baths in the trenches, laid on the artillery to
alert the Russians, and went off to have a bath in
peace and quiet. And how once an elk appeared
between the two half-starved lines, so that the main
war was forgotten in competition to get this monstrous
manna for the pot. . . .

And one will wonder, looking round, what exactly
does the Finn look like? and find he is very various.
Perhaps a tendency to flat high cheekbones, perhaps
the feeling of a straight Greek nose, though a
little fleshier, a little decadent, post-Periclean. And
among the labouring and artisan classes, if you see
them *en masse* in a restaurant, there is a kind of dummy
look—partly due to the high colour, often in red and
white patches on the cheeks, partly to the flat high
moulding of cheekbones, partly to a certain stiffness
of neck and walk.

A great many of the houses in Finland have black
roofs. This may sound funereal—or at least unexcep-
tional. It is neither. The black is matt—and the
effect on a roofline is of a fine sensual exactitude, like
a thick charcoal line left in a painting, good strong

drawing to describe the sky. It gives too, a pleasantly nautical effect, tarred, though the roof may be miles inland against the green. And one further quality comes to mind—the absolute *chic* of black. The great box chimneys made of what might be black suède look very like the suave boxes in which a Parisian *parfumeur* might pack his exquisitely latest scent. Those chimneys, let it be faced, are smart. And again and again in Helsinki's modern suburbs I was confounded with the same impression of smartness—the telegraph poles are painted with an arsenic preservative of the most *recherché* bile-green: and the modern appartment blocks, which elsewhere in Scandinavia look on the whole pretty functionally dull, pass one vaguely like the pages of *Vogue*, for their balconies and façades are painted in contrasting and most subtly chosen colours, strange fawns and pigskin and mole-fur colours, dribbled strawberries and indigoes, exactly as one sees the rich and restrained colours of expensive female accessories on the bag-gloves-and-scarf pages. This feeling is so pervasive that soon even the pine-trees begin to look smart, Prussian-green branches on a coaching-leather trunk.

The Finnish architect is an artist of redoubtable vision. The proportions of fairly plain modern buildings, are generally more imaginative and more gracious than elsewhere in the architecturally conscious North. There are fewer traditions in Finland than in other countries to hold the architect back: he can break new ground more easily, though he usually imposes a sensitive restraint on any new shape conceived. The two main historical edifices in Fin-

land are the plain planked wooden house, undecor-
ated and austerely pleasant, and the neoclassic or
empirestile introduced by men like Engels in the first
years of the nineteenth century. But if there is little
to hold the architect back, he has also the intensely
individual Finnish heart and feeling for nature to
push him forward. Thus, among the normal but
always interesting blocks of offices or flats or hospital
wards there occur such magnificent conceptions as
the Helsinki Stadium. This is as beautiful as a Viking
ship—and indeed, with its pitched sides and its
mast of a tower, it looks a little like an immense
flowing boat set in the green: but more than that it
looks like nothing but itself, an abstraction of weight
and wonder. (These thin tall towers, and similarly
such etiolated pillars as embellish the façade of the
modern parliament building, are a speciality of a
northern people in love with the pine.) Another view
of this stadium may remind one of the clustered
leaning houses of an exaggerated mediaeval street or
of the Cabinet of Dr Caligari—a kind of imposed
architectural madness frozen into sanity. The whole
thing is original; it should never have been called by
such a dull word as stadium.

Near the old capital of Turku stands the modern
Chapel of the Resurrection. It is the cemetery chapel.
The architect insisted on its optimist designation.
One side of the chapel is faced with glass, and the
pews within are placed obliquely, so that the
mourner is half facing the altar and half facing the
pine-wood that grows wild to the chapel's glass wall.
An inspiring, touching effect. And in Salla on the
Arctic circle an unusual church has been built.

Roughly, it is in the form of a sharply pitched roof reaching almost to the ground—so that it rises above the cluster of surrounding houses as a kind of emblem of roof or shelter: but again it is also a satisfying triangular shape in its own right. The list of such architectural successes is endless—mills, factories, hospitals, transport stations all mark the Finn as an aesthete of egregious good taste. He is also eminent in the design of furniture and in the moulding of objects from wood or porcelain or glass: again this is a general Scandinavian or Baltic achievement, but again he seems to rise clear above his neighbours. Helsinki boasts the largest porcelain factory in Europe: not only do its products glaze with an unusual *frisson* the eye of the beholder, but so does its most unnerving name—as ARABIA spells out its desert camel-call on the front of a green-and-buff tram belling past suburbs of granite and spruce.

Finnish locomotives tear through the forests hooting like owls. It is as if they, like their drivers, seek to become again part of nature, to turn into mythical birds as they enter the endless green. Like his Scandinavian neighbours, the Finn is passionately in love with the land. He may build beautiful cities, but at the first opportunity he scuttles out of them. Helsinki on a fine summer's week-end is a city of the dead. Everyone, and not only he who can easily afford it, has some sort of a hut to go to. And not content with this, when a new apartment block goes up within the expanding city, the trees around are not cut down, but space and grass and trees are allowed to

approach the front door: a little landscape of forest
to breath in, rather than a cultivated garden. And
thus one finds such a green and clean industrial city
as Tampere, the big textile centre. It has been said
that here you must search to find a factory: that is
nonsense, the tall red brick chimneys sprout all over
the place, but they are indeed tall, lifting high
what smoke there is, and in between them there is
plenty of leisured green, a weir-drumming river, and
wide and wonderful lakes to either side. It is here
that Lenin first met young Stalin: but it is rather
more to the point that here a nineteenth-century
Scot called Finlayson met the water by which he
chose to build his first textile mill, and from this beginning grew an idyllic industrial centre—absurdly
called the Finnish Manchester. It is a fresh, free-
breathing, green and watery place. But still not
green enough for the Finnish worker, who will always
break for the country at the first opportunity.

When a Finn breaks for the country he likes to go
as far afield as possible, not to lurk in groups near
the city. There is the old story of the Finn who has
built his wooden house deep in the solitude of a
beloved forest. One day a traveller brings news that
another man is building a house some forty or fifty
miles away. The Finn says nothing: only takes up
his knife, and disappears silently in the direction of
the intruder.

The killing is now *démodé*. But the principle holds
good. The Finn loves solitude: and even in company
he still manages to preserve it—by means of the
famous Finnish silence. No one who is not Finnish
can fully understand what goes on during these deep

periods of contemplative silence. To the more volatile foreigner it is unnerving. But it is too easily labelled 'gloomy': and one soon understands that there is little morose or vindicative in such profound quiet; nor is it prompted by such a negative attitude as: 'Why waste words?' It is purer. It is partly his desire to turn over his own thoughts, partly a wish to meditate without thought: and this last is part of the sitting alone with and sympathy with nature—in a people who have different words to describe the differences in the sound of the wind through different kinds of trees, who feel for the music in stones and all the other wilderness magics—and who hence even in the city can from time to time continue to exercise this intensity of simply *being*. Sometimes it seems, looking round in a restaurant, that every second person is an intellectual acutely meditating. There is about this mood an air different from the tense and formal silence of a Swede, or from the actively planning silence of the North German. It will take a day or two for the foreigner to realize this difference, but it is certainly there. As certainly as the opposite fact that the Finn in another mood is equally spirited and remarkably talkative, is seldom self-consciously grave and will laugh and joke and sing and talk wildly for hours. And 'wild' is here a literally apposite word: however poised the Finnish culture, however progressive the social state, a streak of wildness persists.

Paradoxically, this individualist has taken to the co-operative movement more thoroughly than elsewhere in Europe. A sparsely populated country that is comparatively undeveloped has to maintain its head above water in modern conditions. To-day, that head is well above water. One often hears the phrase: 'We're a poor country.' If that is so, then magically they are prosperous too. Standards of living are generally high, restaurants full, building booming, and a high percentage of these northern sun-lovers manage to get abroad to the south for their annual estivation: and one notices small matters—the ample portion of food on a plate; or the rich gold-and-leather binding of an ordinary novel, a luxury that is growing more popular each year at the expense of paper-backs. A set meal in a middle-price restaurant is really filling—say, rice-and-butter cakes followed by roast pike followed by pancakes and cloudberry jam, each course not a plate but a platter-ful. Luxury restaurants naturally keep their prices highish—and one may find such anomalies as 500 *markkaa* for the finest smoked eel and a plate of French sardines for the same price.

The one most noticeable deficiency in the standard of living is in housing. There is a rule in Helsinki and some other towns of no more than one room in the house or apartment per person: if there is a further room available, it must by law be let. But this is a temporary measure occasioned by war, by the voluntary immigration of over 400,000 people from Karelian and other territories lost to Russia and by the absolute scorched earth policy of the retreating German armies, who burned down every single house and hut and village and town in the north before leaving. An ill wind again that has blown good—for the people of this vast northern area have built already, and it seems miraculously, shining new towns where the ashes had scarcely time to cool. The opportunity for complete renovation has been taken and the work done. Rovaniemi, the Lapp capital just below the Arctic circle, is a great gleaming phoenix with concrete feathers. And miles to the north new towns have gone up, go up. And when asked how a 'poor country' can afford so much building, and effect it so quickly, the Finn will answer, with a twinkle at himself: 'By magic.' The twinkle is because he is very tired of the traditional reputation of the Finn for real magic. And the true answer is a combination of sensible help from the government, slogging hard work, individual action, and co-operation with a minimum of fuss. Accustomed to a hard battle with the forest, accustomed through the centuries to this same forest being a battlefield for other people's wars, the Finn has developed an elephantine tenacity: in its immobile way this is something like the echo, in America and the Dominions, of the pioneer spirit: it is a spiritual quality with a fist like a ham, and called *sisu*.

The reputation for the practice of magic (white) seems to have developed from the Lapp shamans of old. Travellers a century or more ago used to circumvent lower Finland and go straight to the Lapp north, then to report on the country mostly in terms of the Lapps. But apart from this, the solitary nature of the Finnish people has always kept them in closer contact than other peoples of Europe with the mysteries of nature than even in Sweden, where love of

Concrete gracing the green—Tilka military hospital

Landsnake peculiar to Finnish waters—Vehoniemi Ridge

Undress affair in
a steam bath

Full Dress at the
National Museum

nature is intense but not *so* intense. There seems no doubt that under such conditions further senses develop—second sight is probably stronger in Finland than elsewhere. I must say 'probably'—for these questions always erect a fence of delicacy round themselves, of their nature they remain impenetrable, they do not like the light. Yet I know a hard-headed London journalist who swears that people in the forest knew of his coming long before he arrived: and a similarly objective Finnish business man told me—but with a certain truculence, and only when I had dragged at him—how he himself had seen an old Karelian woman congeal the blood of an open wound by staring at it. Faith? Magic? Whatever one may call it, it remains one of the most interesting sources of power in the world: relatively unstudied, certainly unharnessed, perhaps disappearing. Pooh? Once we had no telephone.

However, the Finn himself grumbles at this reputation. As he will grumble at the foreigner's predominant interest in the Lapps, as he will grumble also at any Russian qualities attributed to him. It is very understandable. Tucked away in that corner of Europe, Finland has too long been thought too remote. Too easily it is thought of as a vague sort of shadow-place where there are endless forests and people playing dangerous games with knives and keeping endless silence between long vodka-bouts and longer Karelian bear-hunts: somewhere a shaft of light breaks through and shows Nurmi running round an Olympic stadium, somewhere a renowned granite railway station rises. But again the cloud of popular conception closes in . . . and only nowadays, with the established prevalence of air-travel, may the grumble at last be allowed to fade, and a delightful and progressive country permitted no longer to be remote, a whole peculiar people cease to be a geographical phantom. Helsinki is an hour and a half from Stockholm, three from Copenhagen. That is all.

The Finnish civilian flying record is one of the very best in Europe. There is a regular net-work of internal airways, the planes are punctual and comfortable, and in winter they land and take off from frozen airfields as safely as buses: or more safely, since the Finnish bus driver keeps up his time over roads of ice, without chains on his wheels, and seems often to drive for long stretches on the skid. Otherwise, the railroad; or the leisured pleasure of the lake steamer; or the modern Silverline Lake-launches. It is a stirring sight to see a heavy black locomotive come pounding down from the Arctic, its monstrous wood-burning chimney sparking, its whole great body icicle-hung and busy with steam in the frozen air. It is both idyllic and merry to pass the hours on an old lake steamer chugging its summer way across the endless chain of blue lakes. It is lushly exotic to lie back on the luxurious Silverline cushions and watch the northern clarities pass: or to watch from the fields one of these large silvered launches break out of the forest and cross on unseen water the meadow's stillness—like a Thing, a great-eyed wide-mouthed ray-creature nosing swiftly among the moon-daisies for its voracious feed.

By such ordinarily various means the traveller to

Helsinki can get to see in a short while the nearish centres of interest or beauty—say Turku, Porvoo, Hämeenlinna, Punkaharju, Savonlinna, Tampere or the newly built and Americanesque city of Lahti. But these names—how to define them in the mind? Print them in capitals, for a start. Remember that every letter is pronounced, even the 'h' gives a kind of mild hiccup to Lahti. Split long words in half, to rest the eye; accent the first syllable always; roll the 'r's and give the 'k's an Arab kick in the throat. It will sound something like Castilian Spanish, with a pretty fluting of Italian. The Italian feeling comes from an endearing use of the terminal 'i'—so that 'bank' becomes 'pankki' and 'passport' is 'passi' and 'hotel' is 'hotelli' as if everything is called cosily by a pet name. Occasionally you may think you are on some Pacific island, with words of Raratongan shape like RAVINTOLA and RUOKALA, both meaning restaurant. And then with a couple of 'k's you seem to be among eskimos, KALAKUKKO. And with TEATTERI GRILLI—where but somewhere behind the Scala? It is a confounding affair. Of the Finno-Ugrian group, the origins of this odd tongue are shared only by the Estonians and, far South in their isolated pocket, by the Hungarians. Each of these peoples originally migrated from the Urals. It is a curious fact that, although the distant Hungarians and Finns cannot now understand each other, nevertheless a faint feeling of brotherhood persists—a Finn would be likely to root for the Hungarians at a central European football match. Somewhere the Turks come into it, probably via their occupation of Hungary. (Quite by the way, there are oddly a thousand Turks living in Finland, mostly fur-merchants. Which is another awful reason for Helsinki's misnomer, The Stamboul of the North. Not so much by the way is the fact that the difficulty of so strange a language has formed a barrier with the Russians—on the principle that people who do not understand each other maintain a removed, mutual respect.)

As a further complication to the eyes, though a simplification for many northern Europeans, Swedish is in legal usage alongside Finnish—as with street-names, proclamations, many menus. About ten per cent of the population is still Swedish-speaking, the hangover from Sweden's long domination. Previously a rich accumulation of wealth and an attitude of superiority made these Swedish Finns disliked: but that is over, respect for courage and the brotherhood of war has cleared the air. However, the traveller may still be faced with such dizzying problems as, on the menu of a Finnish restaurant, the announcement in Swedish of the presence of Danish Vienna Bread.

TURKU is the former Swedish capital of Finland, only superseded by Helsinki in 1812. It is an old, pleasant and quiet-feeling town, despite the red-lead clangour of ship-yards a few minutes walk downriver. Most of the houses are built of wood and painted cream or the palest of greys or greens beneath black-tarred roofs. Above these rise the solid brick towers of the oldest castle and the oldest cathedral in Finland. But also there rises a new spattering of more modern concrete or red-brick building—

and these give the curious impression of being the truly old and solid remnants set in a sea of temporary wooden hutments.

There are other condiments to pepper the soft geometry of wood—a new concert hall with sides of silver metal rivetted like the fuselage of a giant aircraft, the old green-domed orthodox church squatting like a classic customs house on the market-place. And into the market-place may drive a trap—for customs cling in this sleigh-happy country—drawn by a short brown Finnish horse winking at you through its fringe like a large midinette. But in Turku those on foot—and many feet are students' feet, for this is a university town—turn down towards the river that bisects the town, a place of strolling pleasure lined with trees and bright with boating; and where in the evening, on the grass before the cathedral, in a placid setting ringed with pastel-tinted neo-classic buildings, pink pediments and buff pilasters against the green, open-air concerts are held. Take your coffee here in the nice little wood café on the green, the Pinella, an Ibsenesque pavilion where painters used to talk their pictures away: and there reflect, among such university quietudes with so strong an inland feeling, that really you are on an estuary reaching to the sea and the multitudinous islands scattering the Baltic towards Sweden.

This is the largest archipelago in Europe, and has been famous through the tarred years as the birthplace of a world-renowned race of ocean-going sailing ships. The islands are to Finnish waters what her sixty thousand lakes are to the mainland: one needs some kind of negative photograph to show the true consistency of this land-water inversion.

HÄMEENLINNA lies about an hour and a half by rail north of Helsinki. It is again a pleasant old town of wooden buildings, this time set like so many Finnish towns on the lakeside. It is particularly interesting as the southernmost terminal of the chain-lake water-traffic and the Silverline; as, also, the birthplace of Sibelius, though he is everywhere; as the nearest town to Finland's most ambitious tourist hotel, the Aulanko, a great white skyscraper plumped like a beached liner in a fine old park heady with follies and green rides and an undulating lake: as the site, as a divorced male with glittering eyes informed me, of an old castle used now as a women's prison; as the mother of the nearby village of Hattula with its finely preserved thirteenth-century church, a rich repository of primitive sculpture and frescoes (with Adam and Even preferring to the fig-leaf a switch of birch leaves similar to that used in the modern *sauna*): and with a fine example of the curious tri-form effigies of St. Anne prevalent in Finland—where a miniature infant Christ sits upon the knee of the virgin mother who herself is sitting on the enormous limb of her own mother, a serial effect emphatic of infinity as a hall of mirrors.

One or two fine old wooden manor houses stand in the Hämeenlinna country. Among the birches and the berry-bushes they dream double-eagle dreams through the long white dusks of summer: or take on a special magic in winter, when the low lantern sun gilds the garden snow, fires the windows green, and turns the whitish wooden walls and pillared porticoes to soft lavender—when the old house broods and the passer-by remembers Uncle Vanya or that distant but clearly related Cherry Orchard. At the Aulanko hotel there is an annexe, an old manor set in the park, and in this one may wander and dream among painted walls of oblique-patterned planks, among great old porcelain stoves and the pale dusty conservatory light of a glassed sitting-room leading to the little private garden; the sweet hurt of the loss of days forever past can go no deeper.

SAVONLINNA is away to the east, towards Karelia, nine and a half hours overnight by train from Helsinki. Again a centre for lake steamers plying in all directions. Here there stands a redoubtable round-bastioned border fortress, a big-eyed old monster built long ago by the Swedes: and to the south the Punkaharju Ridge, an eccentric snake of land at places only a few yards broad that runs for over four miles through the lakes. The country up here is wilder and less populated: but at Koli some hundred miles north it is still wilder: and so on, up and up the country. The Finn is very conscious of this hierarchy of wildnesses. To a stranger not used to pine-and-spruce forest country one landscape of trees and lake extending as far as the eye can see seems very much like another. But not to the northerner. I have stood in the vast forest wastes of northern Sweden and thought that nothing could be wilder. Yet the Swedes come over to Finland to a similar forest on the same parallel for their holiday and perceive something extra. Alternatively, the North Karelians come down to Koli for summer softness; to foregather then, paradoxically for the solitary-natured Finn, at this little place with its hilltop hotel and its inspiring views in order to drink and sing and boat the light night through. I questioned the more usual ambition for ever greater wildness, and the answer seems to be a matter of refinement, or rather of engrossment—they see a rougher lie in the skyline of pines, they note how trees have been cracked in the winter by greater frosts, they feel for the heaviness of heavier granite boulders, they can smell out the well-trodden track from the track that leads to one lonely, earth-floored forester's cottage.

LAHTI, two hours by rail from Helsinki, is a new, swiftly built and still building town that spreads its concrete to house thousands of dispossessed Karelians. It has seemed American to American visitors. At present the speed of building outdistances the production of town-maps. Lahti also has an illuminated ski-run—and this raises an interesting conjecture. Finland feels that it cannot compete favourably for the winter sports tourist. The afternoon ends an hour or more earlier than, say, in Austria; and the terrain is on the whole flat, and certainly quite mountainless. The first objection can now be overcome by the illuminated run, with all the torchlit excitement of artificial light against the snow and the forest dark. And otherwise there is somewhere an argument for flattish ski-ing as an altogether different kind of sport: the Finn normally spends more time on skis than his northern neighbours, and he has evolved competitive distance-runs, which have their own gliding pleasure. But what the central European skier misses absolutely by not visiting these norther countries is the magic of a laterally shining

sun. Ski-ing is not only what you do, but also what
you see. And that low sun shining like a giant candle-
flame turns the familiar black or blue and white of
the snowscape to almost a vulgarity of wild, impossible colour—the snow turns gold and pink and
purple and the sky goes green and turquoise and
peacock and the lace-frost on birch-branches and
the snow-draped spruce dazzle and strut like over-
dressed African witch-doctors. The true wonder is
impossible to describe : in the south the sun makes the
snow glitter prettily ; in the north it sets the ice on
fire : in the south one sighs at the loveliness, in the
north one gasps and swears. Someone on these latitudes ought to build a great glass bubble of a cen-
trally heated swimming pool and set it among such
blazing snows : the Riviera would seem dull and
monochrome.

PORVOO is old as Lahti is new. It is a bus-ride
from Helsinki, and an unspoiled example of an old-
fashioned fishing-town—a dawdle of winding streets
and coloured wooden houses clustered on an estuary.
The place where Tsar Alexander I proclaimed the
new Grand Duchy of Finlandia in 1809 and the
place where in the Seurahuone (Society Hotel, but *not*
temperance) one may drink among red-faced rough-
breeched townsmen seated among giant woodstoves
upon which are seated a strange assembly of scarlet
plaster lions advertising an English gin. A nice old
aged-in-the-wood place, an atmosphere.

And back through the forest, through no dark and
awful jungle but a brisk severe woodland that keeps

breaking open onto hidden lakes or wide clearings
of patchwork fields pimpled with beehive stacks,
through a gentle rise and fall of land that reveals the
various and distinct treelines like the long receding
waves of a breeze-chopped sea-swell—back through
the forest to Helsinki.

To do what? To lunch in the Palace Grill overlooking the harbour and the white Great Church and
the gold-bulbed Orthodox Cathedral—off smoked
perch and reindeers' tongues braised in madeira
sauce (difficult for some, like guzzling Bambi's)?
To dine on the pent-house terraces of the Hotel
Vaakuna, or high in the Torni tower with its panorama over the city? To watch a cabaret in the big
round belly of The Fisherman's Cottage, not as
awful as its name, but one of the most beautifully
situated restaurants in the world, luxurious inside as
the luxury outside of wide indolent views over wooded
water? To mambo about the brown, exclusive
Theatre Grill? Or to relax, from so much that is
modern, among the brass hat-pegs and plush and
dark wood of Kämp Hotel, to sleep in a brass bed-
stead achieved via a heartening *art-nouveau* lift, to
enjoy the brocades and even the cigar smoke of a
living past? Or much else . . . to stroll the streets and
watch the blue-smocked women selling flowers on
the quay, or see them at their washing on wooden
piers built out into the water . . . or watch in winter,
among so many cigar-smoking men in high fur hats,
how much naked statuary there is to shiver blue-
black among the icicles, and how Helsinki seems
especially fond of the caryatid—half way up a turn-
of-the-century office building there struggles so often

some patient old grim-beard holding up the rest of
the façade, staring blindly down at the street with
what, *sisu*? . . . and note how above the cornices of
the Great Church black effigies of the saints stand
holding the ice-hung instruments of their own tor-
ture, a sad predicament indeed for Mediterranean
gentlemen . . . or note with delight among the summer trees how advertisement hoardings are restricted
to occasional kiosks and small intermittent hanging
signs—so that you can for once see the city itself, and
these posters become pleasant splashes of colour, like
flower baskets . . . or pick out the minutiae, the occasional black and hooded droshki left over from
tsarist days, or a grave-faced man in a red top-hat
who is nothing madder than a man with a doctorate,
or a sudden apple-green mansard among the black
and sometimes red roofs, or an immense wooden
building-scaffold that in a wood-rich country rises
prolific and tortuous like a Piranesi skyscape con-
structed with giant matchsticks; or enjoy the cour-
tesy of such a notice as 'Please Try not to Smoke', or
the frown of an office built of granite, least placable
of stones . . . and see how in winter the babies carried
in truncated red fleece-bags look like dead starfish,
or in summer how they are up to all hours enjoying
the light nights when sleep never seems so necessary . . . and marvel that in so small a country
there are twenty international societies, the Finnish-
Ethiopian body having fifty members . . . and that the
forehead of Sibelius bore no less than eight vertical
frown marks, where one is enough to give any normal
man the serious look . . . and take care to order
the best coffee, as the next-best can be terrible. . . .

Run your tongue with delight over an excellent
fish, the special grayling of these waters; or burn it
off with *jaloviina*, the cheap false cognac . . . try
Karjalan Paisti, mixed meats braised richly in the
oven, or *piirakka*, which is rice and whipped butter
pasties, or, if you can get it and if you are strong, a
thing called *Kalakukko* from the Savo province, a
brown hump of pastry packed with bacon and little
fish . . . regret that there are so few stand-up bars in
Helsinki and that you must usually sit at a table,
with all the waiting that this may entail, for a drink
. . . regret perhaps, too, that there is a prevalence of
enormous restaurants rather than of small intimate
eating houses (if it is true that a man is most alone in
a crowd, then this is another evocation of the Finn's
desire for solitude; though generally these large restaurants seem to be the increasing order of the nordic
day) . . . and make some attempt, at least, to remember that '*noh*' (*noh-jaa*) can mean 'Yes' and '*ei*' (pronounced 'aye') means 'no' . . . and raise your hands
in horror or clap them with joy to see that here so far
in the Lutheran north the ladies on the stage may
dance with their breasts naked.

This unassuming attitude towards nudity comes
from a liberal rather than libertine temperament—
one remembers that the fully clothed Finnish woman
was the first in Europe to receive the franchise, as
early as 1906. It is also probably partly an after-
effect of the traditional Finnish bathing habit, of the
sauna. To write of Finland without the *sauna* is like
writing about Scotland without pipers, England
without monstrous cooking, or Paris without cafés.
A weekly steam-bath is the rule with all Finns. There

are 500,000 small bath-houses in Finland, and many large public establishments, to serve a population of four million. In the country, the *sauna* is built before the house, the family using it as a living hut while the main edifice is being completed. If possible, the bath-house is erected by the lakeside—so that a cool plunge can immediately follow the steam-heat. A mistake is to confuse this *steam* quality with the wetly vapoured atmosphere of what is called a Russian Bath. The *sauna* is essentially dry. The temperature in the hot room is raised above boiling point—so that when you sweat you hardly see it, it boils off you immediately. Were the air wet, the body could never stand such heat: but dry, it is no more than pleasantly refreshing. The walls should be wood, to absorb moisture. Heat is supplied by birch logs furnaced beneath granite stones. Water is thrown on the stones, and spits instantly into invisible steam which snakes through the air and strikes the body like a quiver of hot darts. And very pleasant too. At the same time, you whisk yourself with a bundle of birch leaves dipped in water—and this action further opens the pores, and sends delicious private eddies of unseen steam over the body; it has nothing whatever to do with a 'birching'. After a quarter of an hour or twenty minutes of heat—a plunge in the cool lake: or if it is winter, a roll in the snow—which never feels harsh or shocking like ice or cold water, but soft, fresh, mousseline. Afterwards, still quite naked, you are washed from head to foot by a female bath attendant. The only real anxiety this provokes is a regret that all through the years of the lavable past you have wasted so much effort washing yourself.

These female shampooers are sometimes quite young or middleaged, and there is nothing severely impersonal about them—they joke and perhaps sexlessly flirt, rather as a nurse might. The story goes that the Frenchman or Italian cannot but react erotically— when a bucket of cold water is the time-honoured remedy. The whole process costs about 200 *markkaa*. As late as the 'thirties, there was still mixed bathing in some of the country *saunat*. Earlier, whole villages would bath naked together. It might well be remembrance of this recent past that explains the reasonably uninhibited attitude of the Finn, though a Lutheran, to the naked idea.

Thus throughout the long north-south country the birch-smoke rises from the little bath-huts . . . far up to the Lappish north. No word has yet been said of Lapland. It is another country, much of it beyond the tree-belt, where dwarf-birches grow only knee-high and reindeer wander over a sponge of moss. It needs an account to itself. Let us only remark that the Finnish Lapp males tend to wear a curious hat like a star with four points, unlike their pom-pommed Swedish relatives: that their dialect is different; but that the rest is about the same—the reindeer-hide tent, the reindeer-raising, the fishing. The census gives two thousand as the figure of resident Finnish Lapps. There are modern hotels set wonderfully among desolate fells and by ancient lunar lakes where the tourist can enjoy the midnight sun and the piquant mosquito. And in the gleaming concrete capital of Rovaniemi, he can taste *poron-käristys* or fire-flared ribs of reindeer, and watch on the passing rapids the log-rolling championships—

that is, sit on a comfortable hotel terrace and watch these extraordinarily agile lumbermen in their yellow pointed boots balance on the hurtling logs, sometimes even disappearing from sight in crevasses of water formed by the roaring rapids. Rapids are also for the touristical shooting in long-boats as far to the south of Lapland as the Suomussalmi district. Or one can just stand about anywhere and flick in the salmon from these abundant waters. As with Sweden and Norway there was once a time when servants refused to work if salmon were given them to eat more than twice a week. Hydro-electric works and export have put an end to so absolute a glut, but the rivers are still rich in fish.

Lapland is far to the north. As always, it is the benevolent old Gulf Stream that makes it at all habitable. But by aeroplane, complete with your Arctic Circle Certificate, you will fly again quickly south, back down the long country, with the Ostrobothnian plains strangely unwooded to the west and with northern Karelia or the 'bark-bread country' to the east (this is a particularly wild part where in the late 'sixties famine reduced the peasants to mix bark with their rye, and which even to-day is an agricultural black spot, only slowly whitening at co-operative suggestion). Down over the endless lakes with their match-stick logs and their scattering of melon-rind row-boats, over forest and forest and the wood, wood, wood which makes up the greatest wealth of this country—until again Helsinki.

And if it is December the Sixth, and if you stand in front of the Great Church on the wide square enclosed so magnificently by unbroken walls of pastel-coloured classic buildings, in each of whose regular windows a candle now shines, and if it is some time after six o'clock on this Day of Independence—then you will see approaching over the snow a procession of some thousands of silent students carrying torches. In front, fluttering like tall ghosts, are borne some forty great white Finnish flags—one for each year of independence since 1917. And on come the students, on and on and on in their thousands by torchlight—*in absolute silence.* No bands, no singing, not a single drum-beat; nor, if there is snow on the ground, the sound of a single footfall. And the crowds lining the pavements are silent too. On and on they come, unregimented but steadily marching in one purposeful direction, until they are all massed in the great wide square—and still the silence is held, and the ghostly flags breath their own white silence, and the whole square is tense with a tremendous quiet that embodies exactly and magnificently the spirit of belief and forbearance and tenacity that has brought this so-called 'young' country through hundreds of years of battle, and which made the world gasp in 1940 when she faced, and held, the weight of vast Russian armies.

Then the silence is broken by the drumming crash, sudden as a cannonade, of voices joined in choral anthem, and a deep music of freedom rises on the winter night.

NORWAY

H

IV

NORWAY

ALONG the granite waves of this enormously long thin country there are two thousand one hundred miles of sea-coast; or, if it is measured as the crab crawls, round each bay and along the coasts of each deep-cutting fjord, the figures may be rearranged to make twelve thousand miles of sea-bound land.

It seems as if the sea had set out deliberately to seduce the Norwegian from his intractable mountains by sending long arms of deep navigable water often as far as a hundred miles into the country—for the fjord is not only a gracious delight to the tourist and his poster, but a haven and highway for a mountain-trapped people.

Result: in the dark ages the Norwegians discovered Vineland, or what we call America, and later on Nansen visited the North and Amundsen the South Pole. Svend Foyn invented the shell-harpoon which revolutionized whaling, Heyerdahl spent one hundred and one days on a balsa-raft drifting between Peru and Polynesia: and a nation of only three and a quarter million people has the third largest mercantile marine service in the world.

But not content with their own 150,000 home-islands stretching far up through polar regions of the north, the Norwegians maintain ten floating islands right across the world in southern polar seas—the floating whale factories, nexus of the largest whaling fleet in existence.

The inland waves, the mountainous granite waves, are not barren: they are vested with vast forests of birch and spruce, Norway's second natural wealth, and as lovely to the eye as to the timberman's axe; but outside the forest the lie of all this land is so precipitous that only three per cent of the earth is properly tillable, and even then the farms often lie on slopes that preclude the easy use of agricultural machinery and make very hard going.

As a figurative device, one may think of Norway as being a giant long-armed lute, with Oslo set down at the base of the ellipse, and the upper arm rising fretted with mountains and ports and then stretching its string-keys round and over to the iron-mines of Kirkenes and the most northerly Russian border. The flight distance from Oslo to Kirkenes is over nine hundred miles: about as far as Oslo-Vienna. The real freight distance—for the railhead ends beneath Bodø and either ships or the Swedish railway must thereafter be used—is far greater. Along the North Sea coast steeply rising to the Arctic there is a studding of centres—Stavanger, Bergen, Trondheim, Bodø, Tromsø, Vadsø and others—all separated by deep-cutting fjords and by mountains and all many ship-miles apart. Up and down this coast express steamers sail regularly, winter and summer. They must, for the sea is the true Norwegian highway. The railhead builds slowly north; but slowly. There are airfields, there are roads. But distances are so great and the terrain so hard that the ship still remains the natural pack-beast of Norway.

To emphasize fully the quality of so mountainous a land, the famous example of the nation's second city, Bergen, must be cited. Until in 1909 the Oslo-Bergen railway was built it was simpler for the Bergenese, cupped by high mountains, to get to Scotland or England in two or three days than to the capital of their own country, then Christiania (Oslo), in five days.

These geographical facts must never be forgotten in any consideration of Norway and the Norwegian. More than anything else they must explain what I have earlier called the athletic brio of the Norwegian. There is something weathery and bluff up here, a roll of gait, a lack of compromise in the eye, a rugged ability and almost a sharpness—both for laughter and for serious purpose. One is tempted to say that even in the capital there is—what?—'a sense of the bucolic'? 'A whiff of the rustic'? But 'bucolic' suggests a drudging ox-eye, and this could never apply to the keen horizon-blue organ of the average Norwegian. And 'rustic' suggests a slow-living life with straw in the hair: and nor can this be applied to the quick-moving man of Norway—one immediately notices how fast a Norwegian walks on the city streets —whose hair, if straw must be considered at all, may seem to be all straw, a most delicate straw of fine ash and gold, for here are most of the true fair-haired people of the North. They walk fast, and they give a free swing to their arms—whereas it is noticeable that a Finn walks with arms hung unswung, as if heavy fur gloves held them down; and a Dane likes to keep his hands deep in trouser-pockets, at deep ease, like the traditional picture of the Dutchman in baggy trousers. So this adds up neither to rustic nor bucolic but definitely to something weather-born, as if the pavements of the town were incidental, as if, whatever the pull of his office-desk or the metropolitan cut of his suit, the Norwegian might be off up a mountain or up on the bridge of a ship in the next few minutes.

One may attempt perfidious simplifications—that these people are like the Swede crossed with the Dane, thoughtful gravity tempered with ease: certainly they are sudden to laugh, and quick to be serious. Or one might say that they approximate the Celts of Scandinavia, westward-looking men who watch their Atlantic islands drown in the last light of each day, who see the final plunge of the sun into another mythical world beyond, and whose mountain magic produced the music of Grieg. But theories overlay the grain of truth that bears them. A people's character derives not from one or two but from multiple reasons.

One may notice in Norway the prevalence of old-fashioned lace curtains, of the enormous cold-table breakfast of meat and fish, of the occasional incidence of a man in a straw hat—and from these one may feel that here is still a strong flavour of the last century, that the will to change is sluggish: but the next moment there intervenes some tower of a concrete and glass office block, or a hydro-electric station dynamited into a granite mountain, or one or other aspect of the extremely twentieth-century manners of a people geared to the open air and athletics and committed to progressive institutions of co-operation and welfare and equalization.

And then one must never forget that the Norwegian shares the same long dark night of winter as his colleagues on these latitudes: and he has his share, too, of the puritan pall that has so extensively sobered the whole of the north, with the broad exception of urban Denmark: but he also has the sea-breeze to blow these away, and a jagged coastline and landline that seems to have kept him spirited beyond such brakes, malevolent or benevolent, on the spirit. And he is, as I have suggested, brisk and energetic: yet careful to see that these virtues are kept proportionate—that his offices, for instance, are closed in summer at three in the afternoon.

Norway only regained her full sovereignty in 1905, after nearly a hundred years of union under the Swedish crown and before that nearly four and a half centuries as part of the Danish Kingdom. This comparatively recent independence still has its reaction. The Norwegians are naturally jealous of a precious new entity. From this comes the myth of a touchy inferiority complex—which I imagine might be more properly construed as a sensibly straight defence-of-rights attitude. There are certainly signs of Norway's pride in the air—most literally in the air, for they are by far the happiest flag-fliers of all these flag-loving northern lands. A closer glance at what seem to be birch-streaked islands of spruce and summer huts on, say, Oslo's fjord, reveals not so much birch as an infestation of white flag-poles. It is untrue that there is a flagpole per house in Norway, but it feels like it; one dreams that the whole lumber trade may be less trade than simple transference, the dark spruce felled in one place only to be set up as a white mast elsewhere. However, this a modern flag-flying, proud and free. There is no Ruritanian contrivance—the parkland round the Oslo palace of the well-loved king is public, one strolls beneath the royal window. And all titles of nobility have been abolished. To match this, but by chance more than design, the uniform of the armed royal guard is topped by a kind of black bowler hat from which depends, like a ironic comment on the old military bravados, a horse-hair plume.

However, another and much older ferocity echoes stronger in Norway than elsewhere in Scandinavia— the presence of the Viking. The dragon's head glittering from the eaves is still reborn in romantic architecture: there are still several of the extraordinary wooden stave churches, built up from the principle of the longboathouse and with storeyed roofs of a pagoda tilt: and then there are the real Viking ships dug up near Oslo fjord, tremendous projects of the shipwright's art and beautiful in themselves as works of art. Because of the presence of these beautiful and dangerous ships, and of the association in one's mind of the scarred and vented map and its fjords, and even of the spindrift echo of 'Norge' in one's ears—the ships' ring of the Viking hammers louder here than elsewhere: though it is not obtrusive.

Viking means creek-man, and so let us contemplate this unique asset of the Norwegian coast—particularly the big creek, the fjord. What exactly *is* a fjord? I had always imagined, rightly enough, a deep inlet of seawater, calmish, between mountains. But what I could never have conceived, and it is difficult to convey this in figures, is the extraordinary length of these waters. On and on and on they wind, ever deeper inland, snaking through arrested tempests of towering granite, like broad rivers spoiling for the source. The longest, Sogne fjord, runs a hundred and twenty-five miles inland. And the source itself, no true source but the cradle of an ancient glacier, makes for a deeply moving moment— moving, in fact, through its very lapse of movement, and gently shallow rather than deep: for from far away on the ruffled sea your ship has sailed through giant dimensions, through an immense trough of fir-soft granite, past farms and pinprick villages and lovely landing-stages that all form part of the life of a waterway which itself seems to have tamed the roaring mountainsides—your slow ship has taken you through a macrocosm that feels, after the reverberating miles, endless. Yet it does end—suddenly and gently it all ends in a single sweet ellipse of green turf! Thereafter—no more water. It is the sigh, this gentle green ending, of a Leviathan pleasantly expired in his bath: or it is like the end of symphony, when a brazen wind of wild music quite suddenly subsides in the breath of some remote, hardly heard note from a single final violin; and like the moment of silence, measurably part of the music, that follows. A hundred miles sounds a small figure to our road-roaring ears: but in these waters it makes for a very different quantity, it is immoderate, immense.

The power of bad art is notorious, the well-used word 'fjord' has a heathery calendar ring to it: do not believe this—as with cities such as Venice, which has so well survived its trial by water-colour, the integral beauties of the fjord remain pristine.

Fjords differ. As with Nerøy fjord, the mountains close in horrendously. Then it is like sailing between walls of rock that will close in and crush, while the water beneath is terribly deep—you are in a rock-split magnified, and there is a melancholy unease, a vertiginous terror, darkly to be enjoyed. Other fjords, like Salten above the Polar circle, meander through fields of Irish-bright green, the mountains lying gently back. Oslo's fjord, over sixty miles from the sea, is a gay unfrowning water wide as a lake and dotted with the flagpoles and hutments of summer joy. Hardanger fjord, approached from Bergen, is the idyll—coursing through mountains majestic but unterrible, and its lower banks white with apple-blossom in the month of May.

Like nature, like other fjords, Hardanger fjord has no recognizably regular dimensions. But as you plod along, with your black-funnelled boat specked like a winter fly on the glassy magnitudes, there is an average breadth of water that feels something like the Thames estuary at Greenwich—though with a further dimension of green trees rising nearly sheer to either side, as high as the water is broad. This dark green fur of big trees is topped with a high frieze of purple and white, mountain-tops that roll along like a rugging of some rich zebra-streaked hide. Dazzling above the green: and below, at eyelevel, the darker green is dadoed with the patchwork emerald and yellow of miniature farms. But they are never miniature to the farmer. He has to till a steep slope and to carry always up and down, with only the help of a stocky mushroom-pink *fjordling* pony. To the alien English eye, these farms look like long green golf-courses turned on their sides—there is a rise and fall of narrow fairway, a bunkering of humps, handkerchief greens, and the wooden homestead becomes a wooden club-house rattling with gin and lockers.

The weather may be blue and fair, the blossom-banks like fallen clouds. But the best days keep the clouds above—so that from time to time the sun can throw a theatrical shaft on the waters and mountain slopes ahead. It is then that the truth flashes home— the quality of such scenery is, exactly, theatrical. Ahead, the mountain-sides fall to the water like a series of diminishing curtains or lateral scenic flats— it is the deep eighteenth-century stage, measured *trompe-l'œuil* built on a magnificent scale with gigantic draperies lit by a spotlight sun.

A column of sunlight picks suddenly on a distant white and black ship—in that instant, charmed with a golden radiance, the ship becomes an isolated dancer on a broad stage of gleaming water, its white deckwork frilled as a tutu. A gull glides far up the green cliffs bright as white thistledown, and rises and falls in immense flight, sound more than bird. There is the stillness too of a theatre—as when heights of impassive stucco and cheese-cloth walls minimize the little movements of the ballet beneath. The water is still, the mountains move only in the pattern the boat makes of them, and even the frequent water-falls, like long marmoreal smears on the green, look motionless—until you draw opposite and these long white lines are seen after all to be alive, creepily moving within themselves like white-skinned snakes, for one is too far away to see clearly the crystal grace of falling water.

At the reasonably unspeedy pace of these fjord ships—thus humbled by time as well as by the great spaces around—these is leisure to think. To be pleased at the old-fashioned black satin and starched cuffs of the white-capped waitress in charge of the saloon; to marvel at the occasional waterside village with its white wood church grey-spired among a huddle of coloured wooden houses; to wonder at such a human pinprick isolated by immensities of water stretching around and the sheer mountain rising above. How, one idly wonders, does anyone choose to be thus locked away? What can anyone do —except sit stunned by mountainous walls on every side? . . . But of course there are daily boats, and timber and other works, and roads hidden in the trees. Yet these villages look more isolated than a similarly small village *up* in the mountains—it is the effect of the mountain wall vertical as a backcloth behind, and of the smooth sheet of water glassing like a stage beforehand; like a stage; theatrical.

Names of the Hardanger villages—Utne, Opedal, Lofthus: and a marvel set magnificently at the end of its arm of water, Ulvik. Here again a white church among the May apple-blossom, the June lilacs; and a stream and a woodmill; and one slight difference—a few gentle green hills to soften the steep and the purple mountains beyond. Sitting in the comfortable Brakenes Hotel you look straight along the fjord,

down a corridor of water whose mountainsides again
fall like receding scenic flats, and in the slow twilight
the water turns as white as the ice streaking the distant peaks above, all then is white and purple, immensely beautiful, theatrical: and nothing moves, so
there is a feeling that something momentous is just
about to happen, something giant and placid and
coldly exotic—as if round the purple mountainside
there *might* come gliding a gigantic swan, its neck
arched high as a hill, silent, huge, majestic, terrible.
. . . But it doesn't, and instead one turns away, moved
and finally frustrated by loveliness of such magnitude, to face the moderate graces of a Franco-
Norwegian dinner.

Bergen lies across the mountains from the Hardanger fjord. For most of its nine hundred years the
city has been cut off from the rest of Norway by the
hard high core of mountains encircling behind: other
Norwegians joke, with a germ of truth, that the citizen of Bergen is a foreigner. The citizen of Bergen
affably agrees. Since historically he has had easier
contact with Scotland and elsewhere than with Oslo,
and since Bergen was a key Hanseatic port, with resident German traders in a powerful position, the Bergenese heart has assuredly a different character—
through architecturally the city does not feel at all
un-Norwegian.

Architecturally, one is impressed by the older
wooden houses rising in tiers up the cupping hillside,
by the celebrated old wharves on the quay, by a complement to architecture of the green hills visible like

outer walls behind. Down in the modern city, one frequently sees the green hillside at the end of a street vista, through an arch, between modern multi-unit blocks of flats or offices. The green is very green, for there is a heavy rainfall, but not so green as this city's misnomer, 'the Norwegian Dublin' suggests. It is not at all like Dublin, nor are the people like Dubliners, though they have the reputation for a particular sense of humour.

Bryggen is the name of the old Hanseatic quay. Along this ranges a number of the original wooden wharf-office-living-quarter buildings agglomerated by the merchants. They are unusually well preserved. Early eighteenth-century constructions, but built on a much earlier principle, they share a deceptive impression given by so many other old wooden buildings—that they were built fairly recently: a result, however much the windows lean, of simple lines and of our own association of wooden houses with temporary huts. But enter the one reserved as a museum —and antiquity is instantly apparent. The light of day recedes, the windows are small, the stairs are narrow and the rooms labyrinthine—it feels as secretive and complex as the soul of the old mercantile guild itself.

There are small lockers where the clerks spent their nights, two to a hole, sitting up asleep on a seaweed mattress: these employees were severely disciplined —on the wall hangs a bull's pizzle whip with which they were corrected—and their whole time was dedicated to the merchant-house, whose surveillance on all liberties was harsh. Anyone who objects to the present day nine-to-six grind should see how these young German traders lived, under monastic, near-military discipline, among the huge barrels, the weighing scales, the booms and cranes and ink of their calling; with keel-hauling to toughen them: yet with who knows what compensatory degree of spiritual dedication?

But Bryggen is not Bergen, although the period is reflected in Bergen's nautical wealth of winding streets and wood-planked houses in the other older parts of the city. A few stops away from Bryggen, with a liner funnel in sight and the lively look that cobbles give a quay, there is the present-day living fish market, where the fish boats tie straight up to the selling pitch and a spirited morning trade is done: and whether the fish-people bargain from sou'wester oilskins or bright new plastic veiling, the old garrulities and the breezes of salt-sea selling brisken the air as always: the fish, too, are much the same.

From the busy bluster of these quays only a few paces take you to the other business of a suavely laid, broad-streeted modern town centre. The flat middle of Bergen's cup was burnt out by a large fire in 1916. Nineteenth-century and earlier civic building suffered most, so that in Bergen the ornate spattering of late Victorian-style architecture found in most towns seems to be missing—together with the atmosphere this conveys. However, there is a little left—for instance the Hotel Bristol with its filigree curtains and fuss of furniture, and a moment in Ole Bull's Plass where two cafés meet and under a wedding-cake façade by a lacey bandstand one may dream back in the company of a grey statue of the famous old fiddler Bull draped in his birch-grove, a wood-sprite waterfall creeping about beneath his bronze boots.

As I was sitting there one drizzly lilac-scented day, my mind on Bull's goloshed past and my eye on a succession of grey plastic mackintoshes passing more immediately by—the cheerful blare of a brass band came banging up the street, and into view marched a procession of brightly uniformed children playing all manner of bright brass instruments. They were small children, many not more than ten years old. Yet they had been provided with such complex devices as trombones and cornets and euphoniums, real ones on a miniature scale; in fact they carried and played all the accoutrement of a real brass band. I sat there and watched five separate miniature bands pass, each dressed in a special bright uniform, long-trousered and forage-capped, electric blue or sky blue or scarlet: one band was a little girl's band, wearing kilts. And all these children played, on these comparatively involved instruments, properly scored march music. Later, as I went further afield, I saw similar children's bands travelling about in the country—in mountain buses, on ferries. How very nice for them! And this is a symbol of the Norwegian (and generally Scandinavian and Finnish) attitude towards children—they dress them in bright colours and give them a wonderful good time on sledges and skis in the snow or on their own good feet on the grasses and sands of summer: all these countries seem to buzz with a bustling child life, there is a kaleidoscope whirr of running colours somewhere beneath eye-level all the time. I heard one woman say: 'It's not a question, as I've heard elsewhere, of

From the funicular above Bergen

The City Hall and Oslo waterfront

Fishing fleet in the Lofotens

getting the children to go out to play: it's a question of ever finding them at any time to come in to eat.' And with all this freedom and early self-reliance, they still manage, marvellously, to have good manners.

Bergen itself has a unique organization for older children—a body called the *Buekorps* which was formed in the middle of the last century by children who wanted to emulate their father's volunteer defence corps and which chose as its weapon the crossbow. What particularly interests the alien eye is that it also chose as a distinctive headgear a Scots bonnet —like those the children saw so often leaning over a ship in the harbour.

And in Bergen cosily set among green mountains —what else? A funicular to run you a heady few minutes up the Fløyen mountain to a restaurant with amazing views of the city and its surrounding land and waterways, a geophysical eyrie: or any of many small walks through the uphill town where you look down through rhododendron and lilac, gifts of the gulf stream, on an arrested storm of roofs of a peculiarly deep and lovely red, red with much black in it, rich as velvet: or see on the flat top of the large square modern post office a sudden sprouting of plastic vermilion—a little house for the post-master: or visit the shipbuilding quays of the Salmon Lake: or Grieg's House, called Troldhaugen, a faerie old glass-porticoed villa set among pines and birch: or take the tram out only a quarter-hour away to bathe, or wander about the old churches and mansions or the white wood houses of what sometimes seems a cosily situated doll's-house town, and ruminate on the very high quantity of pretty girls in Bergen, brisk and round-faced and blue-eyed, somehow also dollish, so that you want to hold them upside down to see whether those blue eyes really move: or pause before a closed box of telephone switchgear in the street and admire the decorative mind of the man who designed its miniature château roof of spire and patterned tiles. And marvel, occasionally, that while Bergen's first claim to world fame is its Navigation School—the second pre-eminence of this tucked-away northern city is, of all things, for researches into the treatment of leprosy.

Between Bergen and Oslo, clinging to precipices and nosing at heights through special snowscreen-tunnels, runs the celebrated scenic Oslo-Bergen railway. Scenic it must be called, because through most of its length of 306 miles the eye is awed and astounded by what goes by outside the good wide observation windows: but it is also a real railway—real enough to have a special cashier's box with a madame in it in the dining car, which is tropically fitted with heavy punkah-louvre propeller fans revolving on the ceiling—a railway with the real purpose of connecting Norway's two largest cities.

At its highest point the line rises to 4,330 feet above sea-level—high above the tree-line. It courses through many different levels and landscapes. At one ecstatic high moment it runs into the wild clear-aired snow-pocked country edging the extraordinary Hardanger plateau. This plateau is a vast stretch of mountain-top heathland that feels, flat to the horizon, like a new mysterious land discovered on top of the world, a nordic mountains-of-the-moonland where the brownish-purple and yellow mosses give way to leaden seas of lake and then close again as if the lake had been a dream, where granite boulders blue as scarabs stare out from a wild froth of river, where weathered snow-screens stand about like giant grey caterpillars chewing the moss—where everything is more like the lost landscape traced in a long brown westering cloud at sunset than this real earth below.

Travelling from Bergen the line worms up to the mountains through precipitous gorges, past the drumming tonnage of giant waterfalls (one of the biggest is off the line, at Fossli, where the water glides to a terrible drop of 300 feet into an enclosed cauldron of rock), until the topmost run is reached and your ears pop with the height and your spirit soars at the mystery of such vast and lonely wind-scoured distances . . . and then gradually down to Geilo, still near the tree-line at 2,650 feet but where corn can be grown, and thence the long descent through green valleys patchworked with handker-chief fields, and on and on past red houses of a richening farmland, past sawmills and lakes and along with a broad river until at the end of an engineering work of magnitude and a soul-turning panoramic experience, there appear the first outer suburbs and the prospect of Oslo stretched beneath.

The Ostban station at Oslo. Simple bleached pink classic façade—might be Toulouse. Trams. Cars. A skyscraper hotel. Above all, the *firm* feeling of a capital terminus and an immediate sensation of stale air. Stale air in this northern, fjord-set Oslo? Only in relation to the clearer air of the hills left behind. Compared with, say, Brussels, Oslo smells like a mountain. But all is relative, and now for the first few minutes Oslo smells of petrol and the used breaths of so many people so suddenly busying about. Yet it is a truly countrified city set on water among virgin hills: and will surely smell so on the following day.

Oslo has often been accounted one of the uglier capitals: but all who say this emphasize the consolation of easily accessible fjordways and the country-side all around. The latter is true: but the former? It depends upon your meaning of 'ugliness'. The largest buildings—the Parliament, the City Hall and Royal Theatre and Palace—hardly prepossess. The neo-romanesque rounded Parliament building is like a pale brick gasworks. The large Royal Palace is a too-blank pale pillared classic weight for its situation—so blank it gives the shrouded effect of a façade with painters forever at work at the undercoat stage. The City Hall is a gigantic *tour-de-force* in dark red brick, towered and castellated, which impresses with size and efficiency but also with some kind of compendious nullity. Go inside this giant (opened officially in 1950) and you will find vast and richly furnished halls decorated with vast and richly furnished murals that depict patriotic and sociologic myths on an intense, earnest scale. After the first dazzled minutes, one may notice that of all the forms of life depicted, laughter is omitted: laughter has no place in this kind of formalized ecstasy.

All these cynosures and a heterogeneous mass of nineteenth- and twentieth-century office buildings form a fairly compact and small workable centre ranged about two natural beauties—a long tree-shaded strolling grassway called Studenterlunden, and the quays of the fjord waters fanning elegantly out to a near horizon of islands and promontories. Usually such compact city-centres have some sort of architectural unity—here there is none, and it is this that the casual eye condemns as ugly. Yet, more deeply on later consideration, one may sense another kind of beauty, or at least a happy affirmative quality, about all this—it has brio, bright energy, and it is exactly its preposterous heterogeny that finally appeals. It is the appeal of sharawaggi let loose on a large, acutely nordic scale. And, in between monuments, one notices that Oslo confects a pretty life at street level—cafés with lemon-yellow lanterns set among the trees, a small cliff made into a big beer-garden overlooking the harbour, a good glint of plate-glass windows everywhere, and one of the most bright and energetic crowds of any city, which is peppered with Oslo's extraordinary wealth of beautiful women.

These cannot be overlooked. How do some cities contrive an especially lovely race of women, almost it seems within their civic limits—Arles, Seville, Siena, Budapest, Oslo? The myth of the Scandinavian blonde becomes true. Watery blue eyes that seem always to be on the point of tears, terribly delicate skins, hair indeed of spun gold, or of sprinkled ash, and often a visionary vacancy of expression, as though they had just a minute before flowered and had not yet noticed the presence of the world about them—one may sit and watch this goddess-life pass in what begins to feel like a sacrificial procession. The men of Oslo, who are not bad-looking themselves, must be congratulated on what at least looks like good fortune.

A place of such varied architecture is naturally rich in enchanting corners. Sit, for instance, at the street café on Karl Johansgate beneath the Tostrup building. Under a hot blue sky the pale-bricked romanesque skyline of the Parliament a few yards across the road gives you a crazy feeling of being really in Italy—or rather, unreally, as if you sat actually within a hard Victorian engraving of a curved Italian castle. Then slew the eye a little around, above the baskets of nasturtiums and violas at your elbow, above the lemon lamps and the parasol, and you have the black façade of that Tostrup building, busy with stone shields and masks and putti and ending in a most extravagant roof—turreted, grotesquely spired and fenced with filigree iron like a French renaissance château built for a witch. And at eye-level, as a proper condiment to all this, there may pass among the ordinary crowd a group of student girls in white dresses and white stockings and black tasselled caps, and a few male students with strange devices, say a red cut-out of a footlong letter K or of an octopus sewn into the backs of their lounge suit jackets, and then a small boy with Lars-from-Mars on his jumper, and a bandsman in a lounge suit carrying a euphonium in one hand and a rolled umbrella in the other, and finally one of those Royal Guards in his epaulettes and plumed bowler hat.

Take a short walk down to the quay, and up a few cliffside feet to the Skansen beer garden. There, under the trees, among what seems like half a thousand tables, among geraniums and the bombazine-and-white waitresses, sit and listen to the music of four grey-suited gentlemen in homburgs blowing cornets and trombones in the shade of a bandstand: and see, over the near water, across little boats and a lazy business of joy-riders and quay-strollers, a whole huge ship, liner-size, raised up dry in a floating dock. That it is in a dock you can rationalize. But where else have you ever seen such a ship showing so much of its underneath, poised in the air? In a toy shop.

It is a big ship, but not as big as the City Hall shadowing like a Brobdingnagian red toy castle the corner of your right eye. Then—what else? A five minute stroll in neighbouring back streets reveals a telling diversity. Above a sort of collection of tents silvery acrobats stand precariously pitched against the white summernight sky (the Oslo Tivoli, a small cheap place, is going on inside); and among older plaster buildings that smell of Christiania, there suddenly appears a low attic saying *Greek Consulate*, charming, diplomacy gone bohemian, flower-based consular flagpoles sprouting from attic tiles; and a little way on, the plate-glass window of a maker of scientific instruments displays a glass jar containing a number of rats, from a pretty little pink foetus through many stages of development up to the final big black hairy adult swimming in spirit, all entitled in Norwegian 'The House Rat', with, in brackets, the unequivocal Latin message *Rattus Rattus*. It is no finicky city that will rise thus above common queasiness.

I write all this to emphasize that the North, and the Norwegian North, is not as smooth as it is popularly portrayed: it is not only a mass of smiling fields peopled by smiling peasant-costumes, nor an orderly grey place filled with energetic Lutheran business-vikings. When I was last in Norway there had just departed a number of West African journalists who had come to witness and report on the cutting off of the heads of cods—to be able to assure their country-folk that the headless *baccalao* received from Norway was in fact fish and not, as was somehow assumed, dried human flesh. All is not plain sailing in the lives of these neo-Vikings. And Oslo, with its energetic beauty, its orderly disorder, epitomizes a general gusto. Indeed this city has so many different facets that very often you feel that perhaps you are somewhere else altogether. For a moment, on the pleasure-boat quays, one is reminded of Marseilles—it is much cleaner but roughly the same shape as the Vieux Port, with Studenterlunden as a kind of horizontal Canebière behind. And where else are there long rows of wooden public seats placed underneath trees (again in Studenterlunden) where people may sit in the evening looking at the passers-by? Palma de Mallorca, Barcelona.

But too surreal an impression must not be given. Extending from this extraordinary centre is the older city of what was Christiania, with quantities of plaster-faced classic houses reminiscent of Copenhagen, and outside this the modern residential ring and suburbs of a younger, growing Oslo. There are

a few beautiful key buildings, such as the copper-
spired brick cathedral on the market-place; and the
old Exchange, white and porticoed in a garden of
green, sudden as a Colonial mansion in a not-too-
Colonial American town. And always one must return to the accessibility of the countryside: one must
take, for instance, the Holmenkollen underground
at the National Theatre, tunnelled only for a few
hundred yards, and climb up and up until within
only twenty minutes, either in winter with your skis
or in summer with your bathing suit, you are out in
high open country that then extends for miles.

This little light railway is an enchantment. The
climb itself is delightful, winding round the gardens
of ascending villas, among birch and spruce woods,
often under the beautiful weeping silver birch, past
rock gardens and rococo terraces, among houses that
spell 'holiday' more than 'town-house'—until the
summit with all free air in your lungs and the city
stretched out remote as an aerial map beneath. Here
at the top stands a large restaurant built of brown
logs and eaved with dragons' heads—a good warm
well-fired rendezvous in winter and an ample, airy,
sunblessed terrace for the long evenings of summer.
On the way there is the famous Holmenkollen Ski-
jump—looking like a big banjo tilted on the hillside,
its belly the bowl-stadium, its arm the fretless skier's
run poised against a concrete tower. The bowl can
hold over 100,000 spectators; the run brings together the greatest international ski champions; the
building itself, and its unique ski-museum, is an
event.

Hills and heights such as Holmenkollen surround

Oslo. Their wildness may very literally be brought home to you by the elk, which sometimes wanders down into a suburban garden—and an elk in the garden is a problem of no inconsiderable weight, it is the largest wild beast in Europe and of a most morose, dissatisfied appearance. Other terrace restaurants occur on neighbouring hills. Across the harbour, there is Ekeberg; and the fine old stepgabled Akershus fortress winking its copper, heavy with ancient stone: and the Maritime Navigation School, looking from a distance like a grey Scottish baronial mansion set against the wet green of a sculpted glen.

Between these eminences extend the blue or grey waters of the fjord, sixty-two miles here from the sea, and gentle, no mountains to frown. Fast modern launches ferry you across, or take you on a round trip. An hour's chug in and out by islands and peninsulas reveals what a paradisial summer of bathing and boating is here at such close hand—and why the offices close at three p.m. As with all these Northern sea cities, there are summer houses dotted everywhere among the pole-like trees and the tree-like flagpoles. Big public bathing beaches supplement a thousand private rock-sea-gardens. Near in to the quays there are two luxurious restaurants piered out on piles, facing each other, glassy palaces on water called the King (Kongen) and the Queen (Drottningen), clubs but open to the paying public. From midwater one may look back and see what is often hidden when you are in the town—extensive deep-sea quays with a weight of masts and funnels and corn elevators and cranes. Yet only a minute or two away from these you are among islanded trees and the lively leisured life of little yachts and bathing. The gazebos of great villas peer from the firs, and miniature lighthouses rise from the water white and black-spired like waterborne chapels. Oskar I's royal residence, Oslo's Osborne, shoots a castellated tower up above the pines of Bygdøy. On a distant darkness of fir-tops sits the ski-jump like a pale white-winged moth at prayer. And lower down there squats an extraordinary triangular building which carves an immediate questionmark across the eye.

This is a special museum house built for the Polar ship *Fram*, which Nansen, Sverdrup, and Amundsen used for polar expeditions, and which has the unusual cachet of having travelled further south and north than any other ship ever. Next door is another museum boathouse containing Heyerdahl's balsaraft, the *Kontiki*. But the Bygdøy peninsula has a third and greater marine presentation—the Viking Ships. They are unique. And apart from all historical association they are very beautiful, as satisfying as good Greek architecture. Indeed, there is some parallel to be felt between the sculptured folds of the peplon and the black drapery of timbers curving up to poop and prow : the heavy ancient planking rises and falls with a lovely lightness, the proportions of its rising curve are mathematically satisfying, the final whorl of the great black swan-neck prow both awes and entrances. The seaworthiness of these ships is notorious : but despite the Viking record for roughness, such ships suggest a remarkable aesthetic feeling among their naval architects. There is a lot about the Vikings that the English forget : we think of them, for instance, as famous sailors—but they were famous horsemen and skiers too. And their great boat-halls have influenced Norwegian architecture, from the old wooden churches to the building of modern cathedrals, such as that at Bodø. However, these ships are the predominant Viking legacy, and on Bygdøy they are beautifully housed among white walls. The *Fram* and the *Kontiki* so near to us in history command study and admiration: but these Viking ships do more than that, not only did they sail into new and un-navigated seas but also into the less chartable regions of pure, abstract beauty.

Back in Oslo proper a further aesthetic question confronts the implacable traveller—the Frogner park and the sculptures of Vigeland. Roughly to recapitulate a well-known story—the Oslo municipality gave the sculptor Vigeland a living and a studio in return for all his work, which they agreed to exhibit perpetually to the public. Vigeland worked hard and fast and devotedly, producing a prodigious amount of statuary during a lifetime that ended only in 1943. So that now an enormous quantity of statues, of fountain-work, of wrought-iron gates and a giant granite monolith of writhing sculptured forms— colloquially known as the pickle-jar without the jar —has been set up in the Frogner Park. Although within the councils of the Municipality many a battle was fought over these works, for which the bill, let alone the aggregate of the citizens' emotion, is enormous—nevertheless the old sculptor's terms have been honoured: so that, apart from aesthetic argument, the park is most certainly a monument to civic honesty. The main theme of these sculptures is the birth-copulation-death cycle, with the naked figures of men and women and children asserting the conflicts and emotions of this fundamental situation. Heavy bronze children stamp and howl, men wrestle with women, a grandfather leads by the hand his child, an advanced foetus stands on its head—the variations are multitudinous. Life is portrayed as an energetic struggle indeed: but, one asks oneself standing before the writhing figures, which are in feeling the products of half-animal half-Teutonic superman—is it not all too brutally emphasized, omitting the nuances that make man's unfortunate predicament endurable? If this is life, is it not life arrested—which approximates death? A portrayal of frozen movement, rather than of moving life? Many critics find a flaming genius within this cold apocalypse, many more feel that here is burning earnestness that will not, in the best circles, wash. But however you feel, nature will intrude. In winter, the dark naked figures shiver beneath hats of snow, noses sharp with icicles: and in summer the growing green surrounds and softens, and there are boats on a lake, and real children dressed in bright colours playing among their dark, life-racked prototypes.

If the darker side of the nordic soul must erupt, rather let it take the Munch way. The works of this painter may be seen elsewhere in Norway—as in the Rasmus Meyer collection at Bergen—but the Oslo National Gallery has a fine roomful. Munch tried to paint profound and deadly emotions—*Jealousy*, an evil melancholy called *Moonshine*, and the *Shriek*. He tried to paint not emotional figures but the emotions *inside* the figures, in a style which now begins to date but always with an enduring depth of feeling. The *Shriek* (or more piercingly in Norwegian, the *Skrik*) shows a bald little figure on a jetty hearing, appalled, a shriek from the sunset and the sea : the little figure has a noseless, mad, tortured awfulness, a figure as terrible as anything else ever painted or seen. It is madness pure, set against nightmare swirls of purple and red and orange sunset : what that figure hears is the sound of the ultimate fingernail drawn across the glass of the soul.

Munch painted much else, including a beautiful Madonna. And in other ways, there is much else in this National Gallery : much landscape—from which one can deduce something of what a Norwegian feels for the scenery of his country and for its strange spiritual call : much academic impressionism—for instance in Christian Krohg and Werenskiold— giving at times as good as its masters. And once again, the academic painting of the last century gives you a truly illustrated picture of a people and how they lived, how in many ways they still live.

Like several other towns, Oslo has its museum park of old houses and shops and old-time life, all brought from their original situation and rebuilt at Bygdøy. Above farm buildings and barns there rises a fine example of a stave church, its wooden-tiled roofs rising tier upon tier to give an oriental appearance, dragon-decorated; this is one of the last members of a large tribe mostly destroyed over the years by fire and the other ravagers of wood. (It is interesting to compare these churches with the wooden churches of distant Rumania—there are many similarities.) And Oslo also has its theatres (very active, naturally, in Ibsenland) its restaurants, its cafés, its dancing and its music-halls. Quite thoroughly there is a Ritz, a Savoy, a Carlton, a Grand and a Bristol Hotel—among many others. The old Kafe Blom is one of the few old-fashioned restaurants left—as is the Stortorvets Gjæstgiveri, a yellow seventeenth-century building with a flowered inner courtyard. There are one or two others but most of Oslo's restaurants are more modern. A good medium of the first class, neither too old nor too new, is Theatre-cafeen, popular among theatrical people and writers. There is a whole list of others—and a revue theatre called the Chat Noir, and a big cabaret restaurant called Regnbuen.

Only certain first-class restaurants may serve spirits, but in others the strong Export beer is a favourite drink—and those who want to race ahead lace it with port, when it is very strong indeed and known as an Oslo Breakfast (the real Oslo Breakfast is the vitamin-rich meal of milk and cheese and bread and local berries which is the free right of every school child). Beer is drunk in the cafés all day long, and until about half past eleven at night. Privately, you may buy as much alcohol of any kind as you like, provided you look sober, in one of the State alcohol shops.

A mixed feeling of disapproval and toleration hangs over the drinker in this city. As usual all over this Northern Spirit Belt there are a number of zig-zagging drunks to be seen every day—all the more clearly for the light nights in summer—and one realizes once again that the long dark winters make alcohol a more dangerous resource than in more temperate lands. In the country, the general rule is only beer, perhaps wine : sometimes nothing. Exceptions are made for the more expensive 'tourist' hotels. On the whole, Oslo has a merry, bustling air. Not so the country—where a rarefied air of peace is at all costs, including that of gaiety, preserved. Over a breezy, almost bubbling nature, the old puritanism prevails.

In the far north, where the all-night sun shines for weeks during the midsummer months, the traveller unused to this may have an odd feeling that it is yesterday afternoon all the time : the light is strange, and suggests the 'pause' period somewhere in mid-afternoon, when time has lost its bearings between meals, when the English champ for the spiritual succour of tea. Unused to the angle of the sun and its curiously reflected light, it is always difficult to sense the time during these strange white nights. Dark double curtains and blinds are needed for sleep, and sometimes a bandage or mask for the eyes : but even thus disguised, the coastal question arises : 'When does a seagull sleep?' as, like a nightmare radio play all gull-cry, these white insomniacs pipe away throughout the night of uneasy dreams.

There is in summer a Midnight Sun Flight, when you leave Oslo sometime after nine and, crossing the Circle in high remote sunlight, descend to the airport of Bodø just after midnight. There a short taxi ride takes you to a high point overlooking the mar-

Vigeland's *Howling Child*, Oslo

...p lassooing
...eindeer

The wooden stave-church at Borgund

Snow and spring blossom, Hardanger Fjord

vellous Lofoten islands that hump a hundred miles out to sea—and you sit down in the gazebo-restaurant to a midnight-luncheon of reindeer-steak.

Otherwise, the way up-country is by rail on the long stretch to Trondheim and thence up across the mountains to Saltdal, still many miles short of Bodø. (To such ports as Narvik, further north, one must take the parallel but longer line lying across the border in Sweden.)

The line from Oslo soon climbs into the mountains: one has the dual climbing sensation of rising in the air and rising up the map—past dragon-eaved viking stations among fir-capped hills and, in winter, fur-capped officials. Past Lillehammer, which is a ski-ing station in winter and in summer the gate-town of the Gudbrandsdal, most popular of the eastern valleys rich in peasant-dress, peasant-painted furniture and other hand crafts. On and on towards the Dovre mountains and plateau—this is another of the fabulous Norwegian train journeys, lulling in summer, momentous in winter. I find I have elsewhere[1] described this winter run: 'Great lakes appeared ice-bound, their miles to the horizon furred with wide-fanning flat snow. Near the shore frozen waves lay ridged like skin under a microscope: logged on the banks piles of fresh stripped wood shone like pigskin. Icicles as thick as tree-trunks hung their green glow from rock ledges, and where waterfalls had been struck solid they hung in rows like monstrous teeth: but cruelly as these were shaped, their glass made music of them: over everything the far-gleaming sun and its greening sky

[1] *The Passionate North.*

played strange tricks of transparency. Such a sun! It hung and travelled all day on the horizon so low that losing heat it grew in complement larger—it gleamed more than shone. It gleamed like a force of great candlepower over the wide land, turning the snow lavender and pink, greening the icicles and greening the sky; and the sky itself receded infinitely, it became more transparent than itself, it provoked in its pale green a visible sense of infinity. Yet this was no true Arctic sun although we were travelling near to the polar circle: it shone not on a barren land, but on a snow-laden gentle place rich with cream-coloured birch and black fir. On such country its low long beam cast everything into a strange clearness—in the same way, though a thousand times clarified, that a lowering sun on a summer's day clears and stills the air just before evening. Everything seemed set in glass, transplendent, motionlessly clear.

'So the day passed as we steamed on through the snows, higher ever north. The sun set early. The last thing I can remember was the passing of a river, swift-flowing water of bottle-green that pooled and snaked down between the rocks and ice and moussed snow, disappearing one knew not whither, and in the cold air smoking.'

Trondheim. Capital of a large area of mid-North Norway. Cathedral town and communications centre. Built on the flat, its large centre of wood-planked houses and shops, two-storeyed and standing back from broad streets, gives the appearance of

a white-painted American colonial township. In the
middle rises the largest wooden building in the entire north, a huge and enchanting classic palace
decorated with wrought iron and with gilded coats
of arms, with a scarlet pediment and with lilac-
curtained windows, the Stiftsgård, a royal family
residence.

This, and three other buildings—the bishop's
palace, the great Norman and Gothic Cathedral,
and the granite-columned palm garden of the Britannia Hotel—comprise the unique architectures of
Trondheim.

O that Britannia! . . . Roll off the iced near-polar
boulevard in your fur coat and in through the doors
of this good old horse-hair and brass hotel—and in
the next moment you will be shaking midwinter
snow off your gloves onto the succulent branch of a
thick green African palm. All manner of creeping
green things snake between the granite gothic
columns, lascivious pink orchids lick you in the eye,
a serpentine creeper stretches out its tendrils towards
the silver on your white table-cloth—as here near
the Arctic you expand sub-tropically before a plate
of creamed elk-balls, ungarnished, too live a suffi-
ciency of vegetable balancement all around.

Such aspects of Trondheim—a stone cathedral in
woodcountry, a white classic city suddenly topping
hundreds of miles of Viking country, a palm garden a
degree or two below the polar circle—these must
finally be sublimated to the port and wharf character of a yellow-trammed fjord town. It is the character of all these Norwegian ports—such as Namsos,
Tromsø, Hammerfest and the few remaining points

north—this air of wood boats and casks and chand-
lers and doorways revealing caverns crammed with
chains and rope and spars and fish. Trondheim is
rich in old wooden warehouses, painted in dark oil-
colours like the deep reds and greens and dark mus-
tards of Flemish painting. Beside these the fishing
boats are drawn in—the unpainted boats. For Norwegian boats are either tarred black, or left with their
yellow-brown planks oiled and lacquered, so that all
the natural graining and knotting of the wood
glistens edibly beneath the white line of painted deck
works. These smacks set to sea with a quiet gleam of
dull yellow, like valuable things, like well-oiled
cricket bats: and it happens, heigh-ho, that the Norwegian word for boat is *båt*.

On the Norwegian railway, shortly after Trondheim, one passes through Hell. And Hell, it is reassur-
ing to note, has a pleasant white church with a pretty
copper steeple.

Above Trondheim there still lie another two-
thirds of the country, sparsely peppered with the
above-mentioned ports, and with Narvik the iron-
port and the Lofoten fisheries and inland the Lapps
and finally the North Cape. Lapp life is much the
same as in other parts of Lapland, with the usual
slight differences of clothing and dialect. The North
Cape itself is a tremendous precipitous cliff of rock,
the last of Europe, and as you care to look at it
either gruesome or magnificent. The whole of this
extreme north is served by excellent express steamers
from Bergen, and by such cultural incursions as the
National Travelling Theatre—but it is a vast and
wild territory, with strange-shaped mountains and

rolling moors and always a rich and beautiful desolation, unhumanized, pure, nearer to mathematics and music than the romance of a painting.

Moments of lovely illogic abound. There is the little island of Røst, the last of the elephantine Lofoten trunk, which is so flat that approaching it by boat the sheep and cottages and the one cow seem to be standing on a mirror of water, a real substantiation of Supervielle's strange village-in-the-sea. And somewhere inland on a wide blue fjord one may come across strange accumulations of *objets trouvés* isolated in the pure panorama—a grey boat curved like a scimitar on brilliantly green grass by a dollish red house, with drying cod laid out on nearby stones like the white eggs of some giant ichneumon troll-fly of these breeding solitudes.

Into the train again at Saltdal—and another stretch of scenic railway to Mo-i-Rana, passing over another mountain plateau of treeless moss where the distant reindeer butt up their scuts like a herd of hares and the polar circle is marked by a little blue globe set like a lost ice-cream stand by the side of the lonely railtracks.

Mo-i-Rana is of particular interest. Here, in country thinly inhabited by poor farmer-fishermen, the authorities chose to build the most modern iron and steel plant in the world. Even Americans come to visit it. It is an extraordinary example of what will be ordinary in the future—the deposition of sudden industry in unsuspecting wilderness. Mo was a pleasant nonentitous fjord village with a cluster of fisher houses and an antlered squire's mansion. Then, after the war, this steel-plant was conceived and begun. Mo became a kind of gold-rush town—but after the present-day pattern, a planned Klondyke. Along with the enormous factory a whole new town of houses, shops, roads and schools went up. So did prices—which, with a shopkeeper's cartel unchecked, remain to-day at sometimes a third above the metropolitan prices of Oslo.

Nevertheless, it is an energetic and contented place. No concessions to the past—the old fishing houses lean decrepit, the wooden pier rots. But, in much wider terms—here is an altogether new romance . . . fishermen taking well to a life of furnaces and smelting . . . one single ex-fisherman spending his days alone in charge of a gigantic hydro-electric transformer station the size of Buckingham Palace built *inside* a nearby mountain . . . the vast plant with its own railway and its giant machinery, its rods of red-hot steel whipping through the mills, its general air of being something too big to be true and about to burst . . . acres and acres of ore and pressure and fire and power, great weights and harsh noise, intransigent imponderables tamed by the hands of a few ex-fishermen and a staff of executive engineers . . . it is the way, with new drive and new military significance, that modern Norway is taking: and for that matter, the rest of the world.

On the skyline rises the high mass of the Svartisen glacier that runs with *black* ice beneath its snow. And above the black ice and the new town and the hangars and stacks of this giant industrial orgy, there presides a further miracle, for in the month of January the sky swarms alive with the Aurora Borealis and moon-high curtains of colour brilliant as stained glass drape themselves right across an enchanted nightdark day.

Through a neighbouring mountain disturbed by the hydro-electric works, an enormously long salmon tunnel has been built to allow the fish to climb round the damming—but no longer anonymously, for each salmon is recorded photo-electrically. And again— that one man deep in his granite palace, inside the mountain, surrounded by shining floors and sound- less doors and the dynamo halls whining and shud- dering in false daylight so deep in the rock: that man sits at a desk in the central control room surrounded by gauges, beneath an alarm bell not built in the superhuman siren-shape one might expect but in- stead as a set of golden tubular bells, lady-like and soft-chiming. And on this solitary man's desk? A large wireless set playing the outside world; and a pipe. He is human.

To earth, and *rakørret*, the raw trout buried in earth for several months to emerge as a kind of fish- gorgonzola, a delicacy of decay much to the Nor- wegian taste. Great fishermen, they have an esoteric taste in fish: the supreme prize, the apex of the ban- quet, being the opposite to rotten *rakørret*—a very fresh cod's head boiled. Otherwise, there is the usual Scandinavian table in Norway, a little rougher than in Sweden and without the Danish prodigality, with a few extras like ptarmigan and sweet brown goat- cheese and outsize mackerel (cheap and very good) and of course a superfluity of salmon and salmon- trout, though the export market keeps the price of these high. There are in Norway over two hundred salmon rivers to tempt the fishermen, and trout can be fished in most of the lakes. The Norwegian's familiarity with his co-patriot fauna is illustrated by an impressive, and true, fisherman's story: that of a foreigner who was playing an extremely large salmon, and could not land it—when from a group of passers-by there stepped a man in a blue suit and bowler-hat, who lifted this hat politely, strode with a gracious 'excuse me' into the river, swiftly embraced the salmon and returned like some Aphrodite of Commuters with his prize clutched to his serge bosom to present it with a norseman's compliments to the foreign fisherman—before disappearing dripping and anonymous on his way.

One must not leave the table without mention of the common stew called *lapskaus*. There are several kinds of this homely dish made with different meats. It is in fact diced potatoes and meat braised together, and extremely good in its rough and cheap and filling way. It occurs everywhere: even when the trains stop for twenty minutes to allow the passengers a wayside lunch, the station buffet may have a basinful of this stuff available. And the word *lapskaus* is again a reminder of Norway's nautical nature—it is the same as lobscouse, the traditional word for a seaman's stew in English and particularly the Liverpool dialect.

But what else of the larger *lapskaus*, the mixed pot of Norway itself? The Jotenheim mountains? The whole question of ski-ing in a country which gave us the word ski (and telemark and slalom)—where in a museum you may see a ski four thousand years old and not dissimilar in pattern to its present-day progeny? Norway has a number of well-developed ski-ing resorts, and as with Sweden and Finland one shares here the entrancing light of the angular northern sun, something that can never be experienced in middle Europe, and a definite compensation for the extra hour or so of lost daylight. And ski-ing by artificial light adds always a further refinement—black night and lamplit snow, starshine and the flowing frosted air—a refinement that will surely, in a country where electricity is cheap, be further developed. Norway's chief attraction for the northern skier is, of course, the many mountain runs higher and steeper than elsewhere on these latitudes.

And what else in this long Norwegian *lapskaus*? The skerries along the west coast, nests of islands calming the North Sea rollers? Or the whole question of the south with its beaches and white fishertowns and such centres as Stavanger and Kristiansand? Or Tromsø, from which so many polar expeditions have set out? Or little Svolvær in the Lofotens? Or strange Haugastøl on its lake on top of the mountain world? Or . . . or . . . or preposterously to suit the preposterous diversity of this long, long country take a boat across the Arctic ocean and land at Svalbard (Spitzbergen) where it all begins again, more fjords, more glaciers, more waterfalls, more skerries, and where if you are energetic you may join the ketch *Havella*, sail even further north to north Svalbard, and take, ultimately in these northern journeys, a pot shot at a polar bear.

INDEX

155

INDEX

INDEX

INDEX

INDEX